100 SELF-DISCOVERY JOURNALING PROMPTS

RICHARD FRENCH

ALSO BY RICHARD FRENCH

NON FICTION

The Art of Journaling

Write Your Way

Advanced Pattern Recognition

The Year End Reflection Guide

100 Self-Discovery Journaling Prompts

100 Mental Health Journaling Prompts

Revelation Explained: Verse by Verse

Proverbs for Profit

Daniel as a Blueprint for Navigating Ethical Dilemmas (2nd Edition)

FICTION

The Convergence: Broken Magic

The Convergence: Restoration

Indie Pen Press
Turning Dreams Into Best Sellers

Indie Pen Press
Seattle, Washington USA
IndiePenPress.com

First Edition: April 2025

Paperback ISBN: 979-8-9919463-7-7

CONTENTS

PREFACE: THE SCIENCE BEHIND SELF-DISCOVERY

You know how sometimes the simplest practices can have the most profound effects. That's what researchers have discovered about journaling. While people have been keeping journals for centuries, modern science has helped us understand why this practice can be so transformative.

THE FASCINATING SCIENCE OF WRITING AND WELL-BEING

When researchers first began studying the effects of personal writing, they discovered something remarkable. People who wrote about their experiences didn't just feel better - their physical health improved, their stress levels dropped, and they gained clearer insight into their lives. Dr. James Pennebaker's groundbreaking research in 1997 showed that writing about emotional experiences could actually strengthen our immune system and help us make sense of life's challenges.

Think about what happens when you write about something that matters to you. Your mind naturally begins to organize the experience. You start noticing patterns you might have missed.

Sometimes, you even find meaning in situations that previously felt confusing or overwhelming. This isn't just your imagination - it's your brain doing what it does best: making sense of your experience.

THE MANY WAYS WE GROW

Different researchers have illuminated various aspects of how writing supports growth. Daniel Kahneman's work helps us understand how journaling can improve our decision making by helping us recognize our natural biases and think more clearly. Carol Dweck's research on the growth mindset shows how writing can help us develop a more empowering relationship with challenges and learning.

The prompts in this book draw from various wells of wisdom:

When we explore questions about identity and authentic expression, we build on Carl Jung's deep insights about how we become more fully ourselves. When we practice mindful awareness in our writing, we're incorporating understandings from Jon Kabat-Zinn's work on mindfulness and Richard Davidson's research on emotional awareness.

Our explorations of purpose and meaning are enriched by Viktor Frankl's profound work on finding meaning in all circumstances, Martin Seligman's research on well-being, and Mihaly Csikszentmihalyi's fascinating studies of flow and optimal experience.

WHAT RESEARCH SHOWS ABOUT REGULAR JOURNALING PRACTICE

Studies consistently show that regular journaling can:

- Help us process emotions more effectively
- Reduce stress and anxiety
- Improve our decision-making
- Enhance our creativity
- Support our overall well-being

Baikie and Wilhelm's (2005) research shows how expressive writing benefits mental health. Smyth and Pennebaker's (2008) study revealed how structured writing exercises can create positive change. Laura King's (2001) research demonstrated how writing about life goals contributes to well-being.

While this book is grounded in research, it is designed for personal exploration rather than clinical purposes. We've transformed insights from psychology, neuroscience, and personal development into practical prompts that invite genuine self-discovery.

Think of these prompts as bridges between scientific understanding and personal experience. They invite you to explore your inner landscape in ways research suggests can be particularly meaningful and growth-promoting.

As you begin this journey, remember that while science helps us understand why journaling works, your experience will be uniquely yours. Let these research-informed prompts guide you gently, but trust your wisdom about what best serves your growth.

What lies ahead is an exploration that countless others—from ancient philosophers to modern researchers—have found profoundly valuable. Yet your journey will be your own, unfolding at your own pace.

Let's begin.

Note: The prompts in this book have been adapted from various research concepts in accordance with fair use principles for educational purposes. While informed by research, they are intended for personal exploration rather than clinical or therapeutic use.

INTRODUCTION: THE TIMELESS JOURNEY OF SELF-DISCOVERY

You know how sometimes the most profound insights come from simply sitting with a blank page and an open heart. This practice of exploring our inner landscape through writing isn't new. Throughout history, remarkable individuals have turned to journaling to understand themselves more deeply and navigate life's complexities with greater wisdom.

Picture Marcus Aurelius, the Roman Emperor, writing by candlelight about his struggles with patience and leadership. Or Virginia Woolf, filling pages with her observations about creativity and the ebb and flow of emotional life. Even Leonardo da Vinci kept notebooks full of questions, discoveries, and reflections about the world around and within him.

These weren't just famous people keeping diaries. They were human beings, like us, using the simple act of writing to understand themselves better. Their journals became trusted companions on their personal journeys, helping them navigate everything from daily challenges to life's biggest questions.

WHY JOURNAL FOR SELF-DISCOVERY?

Consider how a conversation with a good friend can help you see things more clearly. Self-discovery journaling creates the same clarifying dialogue with yourself. It's like having a trusted friend who knows exactly what questions to ask, listens without judgment, and helps you recognize patterns you might otherwise miss.

Research shows what these historical journal-keepers seemed to know intuitively: writing about our inner experience helps us understand ourselves better and navigate life's challenges with more wisdom. Regular journaling reduces stress, increases clarity, and allows us to make decisions that align more closely with our values.

But this isn't about writing perfect entries or profound insights. Sometimes, the most meaningful discoveries come from messy, uncertain reflection. Anne Frank's diary wasn't just a record of historical events. It was a conversation with herself during one of humanity's darkest times, revealing how journaling can help us find light even in shadow.

HOW THIS BOOK WORKS

Think of these prompts as gentle invitations to explore different gardens within yourself. Like having a wise companion who knows just what questions to ask, each prompt opens the door to deeper understanding:

Daily Foundation Prompts help you notice the quiet whispers of your inner wisdom. Weekly Reflection Prompts reveal patterns and connections you might otherwise miss. Monthly Deep Dives illuminate the more extensive seasons of your growth. Situational Prompts offer guidance for life's meaningful moments.

BEGINNING YOUR JOURNEY

As you begin this practice, remember that every great journal keeper starts with a blank page and a willingness to explore. Your journey doesn't need to look like anyone else's. What matters is creating space for your own wisdom to emerge.

Consider what helps you reflect most naturally: a quiet morning with coffee, an evening pause to process the day, a peaceful spot that invites honest reflection, or whatever time and space allow you to be genuinely yourself.

This book offers 100 carefully crafted prompts to support your exploration. Each one is like a different window into understanding yourself more deeply. Through consistent practice:

- You will gain a clearer sense of your authentic self and a deeper understanding of your current values and needs.
- You will also gain greater wisdom in navigating life's challenges and more trust in your inner knowing.

Remember, this journey isn't about reaching a destination or finding perfect answers. It's about developing a richer, more nuanced relationship with yourself by simply showing up with pen and paper, ready to explore whatever emerges.

Let's begin this exploration together. Like all those who have found wisdom through journaling before us, your journey starts with the courage to meet yourself on the page. Your first prompt awaits whenever you're ready to begin.

ONE
BEGINNING YOUR JOURNEY: A GUIDE TO SELF-DISCOVERY JOURNALING

Picture yourself standing at the edge of an unexplored garden. Each path winds through different landscapes of thought and feeling; each flower represents a new understanding waiting to bloom. This is your inner world, rich with insights and discoveries that will gradually reveal themselves through the practice of self-discovery journaling.

Just as a garden doesn't reveal all its treasures at once, self-discovery unfolds naturally over time. Some insights sprout quickly, while others need gentle tending before they emerge. This journey isn't about forcing growth or racing to conclusions. It's about creating space for your authentic self to emerge, one reflection at a time.

Throughout this book, you'll meet two fellow travelers on the path of self-discovery. Sarah began journaling during a time of questioning everything she thought she knew about herself. At 34, she found herself wondering about her choices, her boundaries, and what truly mattered to her. James started his practice at 42, seeking to understand patterns in his relationships and explore parts of himself he had long ignored. Their stories, sometimes messy and always real, will show you that there's no single right way to explore your inner landscape.

"I thought journaling meant writing perfect insights daily," Sarah shares. "But some of my most meaningful discoveries came from messy, uncertain entries where I simply allowed myself to wonder. One morning, I just wrote 'I don't know' over and over until suddenly, tears appeared on the page. That moment of honesty opened up a whole new understanding of what I was really feeling."

James's experience revealed similar truths: "My first entries were stiff and formal like I was writing a report about my day. Then, one evening, while reflecting on a childhood memory, I found myself writing with surprising emotion about experiences I thought I had long since processed. I realized journaling isn't about documenting life. It's about discovering it."

Your journey will be uniquely yours. Some days will bring clarity that takes your breath away, while others might feel more like wandering in a fog. Both experiences hold value and are part of the path.

UNDERSTANDING YOUR TOOLS

Think of the prompts in this book as different keys, each unlocking particular doors within yourself. You'll discover:

Daily Prompts: These gentle morning whispers help you check in with yourself. They allow you to recognize your inner climate, like noticing the day's weather.

Weekly Reflections: These deeper explorations reveal patterns in your life, showing you the themes that weave through your days.

Monthly Deep Dives: These profound conversations with yourself illuminate the larger landscape of your life and help you understand the direction of your journey.

Situational Prompts: These companions arrive for specific moments, offering guidance when life presents particular challenges or opportunities.

CREATING YOUR PRACTICE

Your journaling practice is as individual as you are. While Sarah finds clarity in the early morning silence, James discovers his truths during evening reflection. Some people write pages, others just a few lines. What matters isn't the form but the honesty you bring to it.

Consider each of the elements below as you begin.

Your Time: Choose moments when you naturally feel reflective. This might be:

- Early morning quiet
- Lunch break solitude
- Evening wind-down
- Weekend peaceful moments

Your Space: Create an environment that invites honest reflection.

- A cozy corner with good light
- A peaceful spot in nature

- A quiet cafe before the crowd arrives
- Any place you feel safe to be yourself

Your Tools: Select what feels comfortable and accessible.

- A journal that invites writing
- A pen that flows easily
- Perhaps a warm drink nearby
- Maybe a candle or soft music

WHEN THINGS GET MESSY

The most beautiful gardens have tangled spots and self-discovery is no different. There will be days when the words don't flow easily, when emotions feel too big to capture on paper, or when you'd rather do anything but reflect. These moments aren't failures; they're natural parts of the journey.

Sarah remembers a particularly challenging week: "I kept trying to write about my relationship with my sister, but every time I started, I'd freeze up. Instead of forcing it, I just wrote about feeling stuck. Those entries about resistance revealed more about our relationship than any direct attempt could have."

Remember these gentle possibilities when you find yourself stuck: Return to a previous prompt that felt easier to explore. Write about feeling stuck. Start with simple observations about your immediate surroundings, such as "I notice" or "I wonder" and let your thoughts unfold naturally.

James discovered his own way through difficult moments: "Sometimes I just describe what I see out my window. Other times, I write questions instead of trying to find answers. The pressure lifts when I remember there's no wrong way to do this."

SIGNS YOU'RE GROWING

Growth in self-discovery often looks different than we expect. Rather than measuring progress by the pages you fill or the insights you gain, notice the subtle shifts in how you experience life. You might find yourself pausing before reacting to situations that once triggered immediate responses. Perhaps you're becoming more curious about your own patterns or feeling more compassionate toward yourself.

Sarah noticed her growth in unexpected ways: "It wasn't that I suddenly had everything figured out. Instead, I realized I was becoming more comfortable with not knowing. My questions felt less anxious and more curious. Even my silence felt different, somehow richer, and more intentional."

For James, growth appeared in his relationships: "I started noticing patterns in how I connect with others. Not to judge or change them but to understand with more compassion. This awareness naturally shifted how I show up in relationships, making space for more authentic connections."

YOUR FIRST STEPS

Beginning a journaling practice is like planting a garden one seed at a time. Start small and trust that each entry, however brief, contributes to your growth. Your first week might look something like this:

Choose one time each day for a brief check-in with yourself. Maybe it's morning with your coffee or evening as the day settles. Write for just ten minutes, using whatever prompt speaks to you. Notice which times and places feel most natural for reflection.

You might explore a little deeper as you move into your second week. When you have more time and space, try a weekly reflection prompt. Review your daily entries, not to judge them, but to notice any patterns or themes emerging.

Remember what Sarah learned: "My best insights often came when I stopped trying so hard to be profound. The simple entries, the messy ones, the ones where I thought I had nothing to say, these gradually revealed the most surprising truths."

MOVING FORWARD

Your journey of self-discovery is uniquely yours. While this book offers prompts and guidance, you'll find your own rhythm and way of exploring. Some days, you'll write pages; others, just a few words. Trust that each entry and reflection moment contributes to your understanding.

As James reminds us: "There's no falling behind in self-discovery. Each insight arrives exactly when we're ready to receive it. The key is showing up with curiosity and treating ourselves with gentleness along the way."

Let's begin this exploration together. The prompts await, but first, let's understand how they can serve as doorways to different aspects of self-discovery.

WORKING WITH DIFFERENT TYPES OF PROMPTS

Think of these prompts as conversations you might have with yourself. Some are quick morning check-ins, others like deep talks with a close friend. Let's explore how each type can serve your journey.

Daily Foundation Prompts feel like gentle morning whispers. They help you notice what's present in your inner landscape right now. Sarah found these prompts particularly helpful when starting out: "I used to think I needed to write profound insights every morning. Then, I realized these prompts were simply inviting me to pay attention. Some days, I noticed my dreams, other days, my worries, sometimes just the quality of my breathing. Each observation helped me know myself a little better."

Weekly Reflection Prompts create space for noticing patterns and connections. James describes them as weekly conversations with a wise friend: "These prompts help me step back and see the bigger picture. I often notice themes I missed in my daily entries. Something that seemed random on Tuesday suddenly connects with Friday's insight, revealing a pattern I hadn't recognized before."

Monthly Deep Dives invite you to explore the deeper currents of your life. They're like taking a quiet afternoon to really listen to your heart's whispers. "These longer reflections often surprise me," Sarah shares. "I'll start writing about one thing and discover it connects to memories, dreams, and patterns I hadn't considered before. It's like following a thread that leads to unexpected treasure."

Situational Prompts serve as companions for specific moments in life. They're invaluable when you're navigating challenges, celebrations, or transitions. James found them invaluable during times of change: "When I was struggling with a decision, these prompts helped me understand what was really at stake. They guided me to look beyond the surface and explore what my reaction was truly about."

CREATING SACRED SPACE

Your journal is more than paper and ink. It's a sanctuary for your thoughts, feelings, and discoveries. Creating the right environment for reflection can transform your practice from a task into a ritual you look forward to.

Consider what helps you feel safe and open to exploration. Sarah discovered that lighting a candle signaled to her mind that this was sacred time: "The simple act of striking a match and watching the flame became part of my practice. It created a boundary between my busy life and this quiet space for reflection."

Your sacred space might be physical, such as a comfortable corner, a peaceful garden, or a quiet cafe. It might also be temporal, such as those gentle moments before the house wakes up or the peaceful time after everyone's asleep. James found his space in unexpected moments: "My best reflections often happen during my evening walk. Something about moving my body helps my thoughts flow more freely."

WHEN EMOTIONS RUN DEEP

Self-discovery isn't always comfortable. Sometimes, a prompt touches something tender, or memories surface that carry strong emotions. While challenging, these moments often hold the seeds of profound insight.

Sarah remembers encountering unexpected grief while writing: "I was using a simple prompt about daily gratitude when suddenly I was crying about my grandmother's garden. I hadn't thought about it in years, but there it was, all, this unprocessed loss wrapped up in memories of summer flowers."

When strong emotions arise, remember you can take care of yourself first. Put down the pen if you need to. Write about the emotion itself rather than what triggered it. Return to the prompt another time if today feels too raw. Seek support if you need it. Some discoveries are better made with companionship.

THE PATH AHEAD

As you begin your journaling practice, remember that this journey is about discovery, not perfection. Your entries might be long or short, profound or seemingly simple. Each one is valuable because it represents a moment of showing up for yourself.

James offers this gentle reminder: "Looking back at my early entries, I notice how much I censored myself, trying to write the right things. Gradually, I learned that honest messiness reveals more truth than polished perfection. Now I trust that whatever shows up on the page is exactly what needs to be there."

In the next chapter, we'll explore the Daily Foundation Prompts that will help you begin this journey of self-discovery. But for now, take a moment to appreciate the step you're taking. Opening to self-discovery takes courage. Trust that you have everything you need to begin.

Remember Sarah's words: "The blank page isn't waiting for perfection. It's simply offering space for your truth to unfold, one word at a time."

STEPPING INTO PRACTICE

Before we move into the daily prompts that will begin your journey, take a moment to appreciate where you are right now. You're standing at the threshold of deeper self-understanding. Like Sarah and James, you might feel both excited and uncertain. This mix of emotions is natural and welcome. It signals you're ready to explore.

"I remember staring at that first blank page," Sarah reflects. "It felt both inviting and intimidating. Now, I realize that uncertainty itself was the perfect place to begin. Every honest word written becomes a stepping stone to understanding, even if we can't see where the path leads at first."

James adds this gentle reminder: "The prompts in the next chapter aren't tasks to complete. They're invitations to listen to yourself. Some days, you'll want to dive deep; others, you'll simply dip your toes in. Trust your instincts about what feels right for you."

As we move into *Chapter 2: Daily Foundation Prompts*, remember that each small step builds your capacity for self-discovery. These daily reflections will help you develop a natural rhythm of self-awareness. They create quiet moments in your day to hear your own wisdom.

Consider these upcoming prompts as friendly morning questions, gentle ways to check in with yourself as you build your practice. They'll help you notice what you think, feel, need, and what patterns shape your days.

Sarah shares: "The daily prompts became like faithful companions. They helped me recognize subtle shifts in my inner weather. Sometimes, a simple question about what I noticed in the morning revealed insights into deeper patterns in my life."

Turn the page when you're ready. Your journey of self-discovery awaits one reflection at a time.

TWO
BEGINNING YOUR PRACTICE

L ike the first light of dawn revealing the world anew, daily reflection illuminates the quiet truths of your inner landscape. These foundation prompts serve as gentle morning questions, inviting you to notice what stirs within as you begin each day.

Think of these seven prompts as trusted companions on your journey of self-discovery. Each one opens a different window into understanding yourself, offering fresh perspectives on your thoughts, feelings, and patterns. You might find yourself drawn to specific prompts more than others. Trust this natural attraction. It often signals where the richest insights await.

DAILY FOUNDATION PROMPT 1: WHAT EMOTIONS SHAPE YOUR ENERGY TODAY?

Emotions color our world, influencing how we see ourselves and interact with others. This prompt invites you to recognize the subtle currents of feeling that flow through your day. Sometimes, you'll notice obvious waves of joy or worry. Other times, you might discover quieter undercurrents you hadn't recognized before.

Sarah discovered how this simple question revealed hidden patterns: "One morning, I noticed a familiar flutter of anxiety as I prepared for a friend's visit. Instead of pushing past it, I stayed with the feeling. Beneath the surface nervousness, I found a deeper worry about being truly seen. This recognition helped me understand why I often kept conversations light and casual, avoiding deeper connection."

James found this prompt particularly helpful during challenging times: "I woke feeling heavy with sadness about a friend's illness. My first instinct was to push the feeling aside and focus on tasks. But naming the emotion permitted me to honor my sadness and care for my friend. Acknowledging these feelings helped me move through the day more authentically."

When working with this prompt, let yourself notice without judgment. Your emotions aren't problems to solve but messengers offering insights about what matters to you. Some days, you might write pages about a complex emotional landscape. On other mornings, you might note "tired," "peaceful," or "not sure." Each response is valid and offers its own form of self-understanding.

Consider questions like: What's the first feeling you notice as you wake? Where do you feel emotions in your body? How do different feelings influence your energy? What emotions linger from yesterday?

Remember, this isn't about changing or fixing your emotions. It's about developing a friendly curiosity toward your inner experience. Sarah notes: "Over time, I've learned that acknowledging my feelings, even the uncomfortable ones, creates more space for genuine presence in my life."

DAILY FOUNDATION PROMPT 2: WHAT DOES THIS CHOICE REVEAL ABOUT WHAT MATTERS TO ME?

Every day brings moments of choice. Some feel significant, while others seem routine, yet each decision carries whispers of our deeper values and truths. This prompt invites you to notice what your choices reveal about what truly matters to you.

Sarah found unexpected insight in a simple morning decision: "I noticed myself rushing through breakfast to answer early emails. Pausing to reflect, I realized this wasn't about productivity. It spoke to an old belief that being constantly available makes me valuable. This awareness helped me recognize how often I sacrifice self-care for external validation. The next morning, I chose to eat slowly, savoring my coffee and the quiet. This small act of self-respect felt surprisingly powerful."

James discovered layers of meaning in his weekend routines: "I had always declined invitations to Sunday afternoon gatherings, claiming I needed time to prepare for the week. When I explored this pattern more deeply, I recognized that my introverted nature truly needs this quiet space to feel grounded. Understanding this wasn't about being antisocial but about honoring my natural rhythms helped me set boundaries with more confidence."

Your daily choices might reveal what you genuinely value versus what you think you should value, where you naturally invest your energy, how you balance different needs and desires, and which voices guide your decisions, your own or others.

As you work with this prompt, notice both the choices you make and the ones you avoid. Sometimes what we choose not to do reveals as much as what we do.

DAILY FOUNDATION PROMPT 3: WHERE DO YOU FIND CLARITY TODAY?

Clarity often arrives like sunlight through parting clouds appearing in unexpected moments and places. This prompt encourages you to notice when and where your mind feels most clear, your heart most certain, and your path most evident.

"I used to think clarity meant having everything figured out," Sarah shares. "Then, one morning, walking in my neighborhood, I noticed how peaceful I felt watching leaves dance in the wind. In that simple moment, I understood something about my need for constant motion. Sometimes clarity comes not from analyzing but from simply being present."

James found clarity in moments of contrast: "During my morning writing, I noticed how different my mind feels before engaging with the world's noise. There's a natural wisdom in this quiet time before I start responding to everyone else's needs and ideas. This recognition helped me protect these early hours for reflection."

Clarity might arrive through a moment of quiet observation, a conversation that shifts your perspective, a physical movement that settles your mind, nature's simple teachings, or an unexpected memory or dream.

Remember that clarity doesn't always mean certainty about the whole path forward. Sometimes, it's a gentle knowing about just the next step or a quiet understanding of what no longer serves you.

"The more I work with this prompt," Sarah reflects, "the more I recognize that clarity often comes wrapped in simplicity. It's less about figuring everything out and more about noticing what already feels true."

DAILY FOUNDATION PROMPT 4: WHAT GROWTH EDGE INVITES YOUR ATTENTION?

Growth often whispers to us in moments of gentle discomfort, calling us toward new possibilities. This prompt encourages you to notice where life might be inviting you to stretch, learn, or expand beyond familiar patterns.

Sarah discovered her growth edge in an unexpected place: "I noticed how often I changed the subject when friends asked about my creative projects. This wasn't about privacy. It was about my fear of being seen as someone who takes her dreams seriously. My growth edge appeared in that space between wanting to share and wanting to hide. Each small step toward speaking openly about my aspirations helped me claim them more fully."

James found his growth calling through physical sensations: "I realized I tense up whenever someone disagrees with me. Even mild differences of opinion trigger an urge to defend or withdraw. This awareness opened a new territory for growth. Could I stay present and curious when others see things differently? Could I welcome diverse perspectives as opportunities for understanding rather than threats to my viewpoint?"

Your growth edge might appear as a recurring situation that consistently challenges you, a desire that feels both exciting and frightening, a pattern you notice but haven't yet been ready to address, a quiet knowing that something wants to change.

Remember that growth edges aren't problems to fix but doorways to deeper understanding. As Sarah notes: "The invitation usually feels both uncomfortable and somehow right. Like something in me has been waiting to explore this territory."

DAILY FOUNDATION PROMPT 5: WHAT CONVERSATION SEEKS EXPRESSION?

Sometimes, the most important conversations happen first within ourselves. This prompt invites you to notice what you want to acknowledge, express, or explore through dialogue, whether with yourself or others.

"I kept thinking about my sister," Sarah shares. "Not about our usual surface chatter, but about things left unsaid since childhood. I realized this wasn't just about missing her. Something deeper wanted to be spoken between us. When I finally called her, the conversation opened places in both our hearts that had been waiting years for this moment."

James recognized an internal dialogue that needed attention: "I noticed myself having imaginary arguments in my head with my father. Rather than dismiss these thoughts, I sat with them. What needed to be said? What needed to be heard? Writing these conversations in my journal helped me understand both his perspective and my own more clearly."

A conversation might be seeking expression when you notice Thoughts that keep returning about a person or situation, feelings that surface around certain topics, dreams featuring dialogue or communication, or a sense of unfinished business in a relationship.

Not every conversation that seeks expression needs to happen externally. Sometimes writing a letter you never send or having a dialogue in your journal provides the understanding you need. As James reflects: "Some conversations are about finding clarity within myself rather than changing something with someone else."

DAILY FOUNDATION PROMPT 6: WHAT PATTERN ASKS FOR YOUR ATTENTION?

Patterns in our lives often speak softly at first, like a gentle tap on the shoulder. They reveal themselves through repeated experiences, familiar feelings, or recurring situations. This prompt invites you to notice these rhythms with curiosity rather than judgment.

"I started noticing how often I apologize," Sarah shares. "Not for actual mistakes, but for simply taking up space. For having needs. For expressing opinions. At first, this pattern felt over- whelming to recognize. But simply noticing it with gentleness, without rushing to fix it, opened space for a deeper under- standing of where this habit came from and what it might be protecting."

James discovered his patterns through physical sensations: "I realized I hold my breath whenever someone asks me what I want. This pattern showed up in small moments, like choosing where to eat and in larger decisions about my life direction. Recognizing this connection between breath and choice helped me understand how often I disconnect from my own desires to avoid disappointing others."

Patterns might reveal themselves through repeated emotional responses to similar situations, physical sensations that arise in certain contexts, familiar roles you find yourself playing in relationships, or recurring themes in your daily reflections.

Remember that recognizing a pattern doesn't mean you must immediately change it. Sometimes, understanding grows slowly, like a photograph gradually developing. As Sarah notes: "Just witnessing my patterns with compassion has created subtle but meaningful shifts in how I show up for myself."

DAILY FOUNDATION PROMPT 7: WHAT POSSIBILITY WHISPERS TO YOU TODAY?

Each day carries seeds of potential, quiet invitations toward new ways of being. This prompt encourages you to listen for the gentle whispers of possibility that might easily go unheard in the noise of daily life.

"Sometimes possibility arrives as a quiet wondering," Sarah reflects. "What if I started that creative project I keep dreaming about? What if I trusted my intuition more? These whispers often feel both exciting and vulnerable. I'm learning that this combination of anticipation and uncertainty often signals something worth exploring."

James found a possibility in unexpected places: "I noticed how alive I feel when sharing stories about my travels. Initially, I dismissed this as simple nostalgia. But listening more closely, I recognized a deeper invitation to bring more adventure and spontaneity into my current life. Small changes, like taking new routes home or striking up conversations with strangers, have opened surprising doors."

A possibility might arrive as a persistent daydream that keeps returning, a sense of energy around certain ideas or activities, a quiet longing for something different or an unexpected moment of joy that hints at more.

"Working with this prompt," Sarah shares, "has taught me that possibility doesn't always announce itself dramatically. Sometimes it's as subtle as a shift in perspective, a moment of wondering 'what if' or a small choice to do something differently."

These daily foundation prompts offer different doorways into self-discovery. Some days, you might find rich insight through one prompt, while other days, you might feel quieter and more observational. Both experiences contribute to your understanding. As you continue working with these prompts, you'll develop your own rhythm of reflection, your own way of listening to the wisdom that emerges through daily practice.

Remember that self-discovery isn't about reaching a destination but about developing a deeper relationship with yourself. Each reflection, whether profound or seemingly simple, adds to your understanding. Trust that the patterns, insights, and possibilities will reveal themselves in their own time through your patient attention and gentle curiosity.

WORKING WITH THESE PROMPTS OVER TIME

Like tending a garden through changing seasons, your relationship with these prompts will evolve naturally. Some prompts might feel immediately inviting, while others require patience before yielding their insights. This evolution is not only natural but valuable, revealing different aspects of yourself as you grow.

Sarah discovered how her practice deepened over the months: "At first, I tried to use every prompt every day, treating them like tasks to complete. This left me feeling scattered and shallow. Then, I learned to listen for which prompt called to me each morning. For some weeks, I stayed with the same prompt, discovering new layers each time. Other times, I moved between prompts as my inner landscape shifted. The key was trusting my own rhythm."

James found value in periodically reviewing his entries: "Looking back over three months of daily reflections, I noticed patterns I couldn't see in the moment. Certain themes kept emerging through different prompts. My relationship with uncertainty showed up whether I was exploring emotions, examining choices, or considering possibilities. This broader view helped me understand how different aspects of my experience connected."

Consider the gentle suggestions below for developing your practice.

Stay curious about how different prompts resonate at different times. Your natural attraction or resistance to certain prompts often carries valuable information about what's ready to be explored.

Allow your responses to vary in length and depth. Some days might bring flowing paragraphs of insight, others just a few honest words. Both serve your journey of self-discovery.

Notice how insights build upon each other. An observation about emotion today might illuminate a pattern you recognize next week, which could reveal a possibility you hadn't considered before.

Trust that understanding develops in its own time. Some insights need to simmer slowly before revealing their full meaning. Others might shift and evolve as you grow.

MOVING INTO WEEKLY REFLECTION

As you develop comfort with daily reflection, you might notice larger patterns and themes emerging in your awareness. This natural evolution leads us to our next chapter, where we'll explore Weekly Reflection Prompts that help you recognize the broader rhythms of your inner life.

Think of daily prompts as gathering drops of water. Weekly reflection allows you to step back and notice the streams and rivers they form. These wider perspectives reveal how individual moments connect into meaningful patterns.

Sarah describes this transition: "Daily prompts helped me develop a regular practice of self-awareness. But when I began working with weekly reflections, I discovered how these daily insights wove together into a larger understanding. Patterns I couldn't see day by day became clear when viewed through a wider lens."

James found that daily practice naturally prepared him for deeper exploration: "The more I worked with daily prompts, the more I wanted to understand the connections between different experiences. Weekly reflection provided space to see these connections and explore their meaning more fully."

As we move into Chapter 3, we'll discover how stepping back for a broader view can reveal new insights about your journey. The patient attention you've developed through daily practice will serve as a foundation for this deeper exploration.

Remember, each person's journey of self-discovery unfolds uniquely. Trust your intuition about when to stay with daily reflection and when to expand into weekly practice. Both serve your growing understanding of yourself.

THREE
DISCOVERING DEEPER PATTERNS

Imagine walking a familiar path each day, noticing individual flowers, stones, and changes in the landscape. Then, once a week, you climb to a gentle hill overlooking this path. From this new perspective, you see how these daily observations connect to larger patterns. This is the relationship between daily journaling and weekly reflection.

Weekly reflection doesn't replace your daily practice. Instead, it offers a wider lens through which to view your journey. Think of daily prompts as gathering precious stones, while weekly reflection helps you arrange them into meaningful patterns.

CREATING SPACE FOR WEEKLY PRACTICE

Sarah discovered the natural rhythm of combining daily and weekly reflection: "I keep my morning journaling practice sacred. Those quiet moments with coffee and my journal still anchor my days. But Sunday evenings have become a special time when I curl up in my favorite chair, review my daily entries, and let myself notice the larger stories emerging. Sometimes patterns jump out immediately. Other times, simply sitting with the week's experiences reveals connections I hadn't noticed before."

James found his weekly rhythm differently: "Friday afternoons work best for me. After the week's activities settle, I take my journal to a quiet café. Having that physical separation helps me step back and see the bigger picture. I still write every morning, but this weekly pause helps me understand how my daily insights connect to deeper themes in my life."

THE DANCE OF DAILY AND WEEKLY PRACTICE

Your daily journaling builds a foundation of self-awareness, capturing moments, feelings, and observations as they arise. Weekly reflection then invites you to notice how these pieces fit together.

Some ways to weave these practices:

Keep your daily writing fresh and spontaneous. Let each morning's reflection flow naturally without worrying about weekly themes or patterns.

Choose a weekly time that feels spacious and nurturing. Whether it's Sunday morning with tea, Friday afternoon in nature, or Saturday evening by candlelight, make this time different from your daily practice.

Begin your weekly reflection by gently reviewing your daily entries. Notice what stands out, what patterns emerge, and what themes whisper for attention.

Trust that some weekly reflections will feel deeper than others.

Like daily journaling, this practice has its own natural rhythm of insight and integration.

Let's explore the weekly prompts that will help you discover these deeper patterns in your journey of self-discovery.

WEEKLY REFLECTION PROMPT 1: WHAT PATTERNS SHAPED YOUR WEEK?

Patterns in our lives often speak in whispers. A feeling that returns in certain situations. A reaction that plays out with different people. A hope that keeps nudging at your awareness. This prompt invites you to notice these gentle repetitions and explore what they might be trying to tell you.

Sarah discovered an unexpected pattern during her weekly reflection: "Looking through my daily entries, I noticed how often I described feeling 'just a little tired' when plans with friends approached. At first, this seemed simple enough. Life is busy, after all. But sitting with this pattern revealed something deeper. The tiredness appeared most often before gatherings where I felt pressure to be 'on,' to entertain or impress. This recognition helped me understand how much energy I spend maintaining a particular image, even with friends. It opened questions about where I might practice being more authentically myself."

James found his patterns through physical sensations: "Reading through my week's observations, I realized my shoulders tense every time I need to assert a boundary. Whether saying no to additional commitments or expressing a different opinion, this physical pattern signaled how uncomfortable I still feel about claiming my own space. Understanding this connection helps me recognize when I'm abandoning my needs to keep peace."

27

When exploring patterns in your week, consider:

What situations repeatedly stirred certain emotions? Sometimes the same feeling appears in seemingly different situations, revealing a hidden connection.

Where did you feel most naturally yourself? These moments often point to authentic patterns worth nurturing.

What challenged you more than once? Recurring challenges might reveal both growth edges and established strengths.

Which thoughts kept returning? Even quiet wonderings can signal meaningful patterns seeking attention.

"The beauty of weekly pattern recognition," Sarah reflects, "is that it transforms what might feel like random experiences into meaningful insight. A moment of hesitation on Tuesday, a dream on Thursday, and a memory on Saturday might weave together into a clear message about what needs attention in my life."

Remember that patterns aren't problems to solve. They're more like threads in the tapestry of your life, each one contributing to the larger picture of who you are and who you're becoming. Some patterns might invite change, while others simply ask to be understood with compassion.

JAMES SHARES, "SOMETIMES, JUST RECOGNIZING A PATTERN BRINGS A natural shift. Other patterns seem to need longer holding, like watching a photo develop slowly. I'm learning to trust this timing, to let understanding emerge in its own way."

Consider keeping notes about patterns that emerge during your weekly reflection. Over time, you might notice larger patterns in the patterns, deeper rhythms that reveal themselves through patient attention to your inner life.

WEEKLY REFLECTION PROMPT 2: WHERE DID TRUST DEEPEN?

You know those moments when trust appears like morning light through your window? Not because you planned it but because something genuine broke through the usual patterns. This prompt invites you to notice where trust might be quietly growing in your life.

Sarah noticed a subtle shift: "Reading through my entries, I realized something changed after I finally shared with my sister how much her childhood teasing had hurt me. I had been carrying this weight for years, afraid that speaking up would damage our relationship. When I finally opened up, there was this moment of complete vulnerability. Her response wasn't perfect, but something between us softened. We both started breathing a little easier. Later, she texted to thank me, saying my honesty helped her see herself differently, too. I'm learning that trust grows not from pretending everything is fine but from sharing our messy truths."

James discovered trust in uncertainty: "The moment that keeps drawing my attention happened during a conversation with my teenage son. Instead of jumping in with advice about his friendship struggles, I admitted that I still sometimes feel unsure about navigating relationships. I worried this would make him lose confidence in me. Instead, our conversation opened up in this beautiful way because we were both just being human together. There's something here about authentic presence that I want to understand better."

Isn't it interesting how trust often grows in these unplanned moments of honesty? It's like watching a garden bloom, not because you demanded flowers but because you created the right conditions. Those times when we dare to let our guard down, even a little, often matter more than grand gestures or carefully planned conversations. Sometimes the very thing we think might break trust, like admitting we don't have it all figured out, creates the perfect soil for deeper connection to grow.

This week, notice the quiet places where trust might be inviting you closer. Maybe it's in a relationship that feels ready for more honesty. Or perhaps it's in your relationship with yourself, in those moments when you're learning to trust your own knowing.

WEEKLY REFLECTION PROMPT 3: WHAT BOUNDARY FEELS LIKE SELF-CARE?

Have you noticed how the healthiest gardens have thoughtful borders? They are not walls that isolate but spaces that allow things to grow in their own way. Our lives are like that, too. Sometimes, what we call boundaries are really just ways of honoring what feels true and nurturing to us.

Sarah encountered a gentle revelation: "Looking through my week, I notice how that word 'boundary' still makes my stomach tighten. But something shifted when I started saying no to evening phone calls. At first, I felt this wave of guilt, like I was letting everyone down. Then, I noticed something surprising. Those quiet evenings weren't just about getting more rest. They became this sacred time where I could hear my own thoughts again. I'm beginning to understand that boundaries aren't just about keeping things out. They're about making space for what matters most."

James found himself questioning old patterns: "I've always been the friend everyone could call anytime, day or night. This week, for the first time, I tried something different. I let people know I needed Saturday mornings for myself. The guilt was intense at first. But as I sat with my coffee that first quiet Saturday, watching the sunrise, I realized something. When I stopped being constantly available, I could actually be more present in my relationships. I'm curious now about what other boundaries might actually help me show up more fully in my life."

You know that feeling when you finally give yourself permission to need what you need? It's like taking a deep breath after holding it for too long. Boundaries aren't about building walls. They're more like creating a cozy space where your authentic self can settle in and get comfortable. Sometimes the very things we worry might push people away actually invite deeper, more genuine connections.

This week, notice where your heart might be asking for a little more space, a little more protection. What would it feel like to honor those quiet requests?

WEEKLY REFLECTION PROMPT 4: WHAT POSSIBILITY BECKONS?

Remember when you were little, and anything felt possible? That sense of possibility doesn't vanish as we grow up. It just gets quieter and more subtle, like the first hints of spring stirring beneath winter soil. This prompt invites you to listen for those gentle whispers of what could be.

Sarah found herself surprised by persistent wonderings: "Reading through my entries this week, I keep finding traces of something I haven't been ready to name. Every time I help a friend work through a difficult situation, something comes alive in me. Not just satisfaction but this spark of genuine joy. It feels almost too tender to look at directly, but what if this is showing me something about my path? What if all those psychology books I read 'just for fun' weren't random at all? I'm not ready to make any big moves, but just acknowledging this interest feels both terrifying and somehow right."

James discovered possibility in unlikely places: "The moments that keep glowing in my mind aren't what I expected. It's not the big achievements or planned activities. Instead, I notice how alive I feel during spontaneous conversations with strangers at the farmers market or when sharing stories with my neighbors. There's something here about connection and community that keeps tugging at my awareness. I'm beginning to wonder what might happen if I created more space for these unplanned moments of genuine meeting."

Isn't it interesting how possibility often shows up wrapped in ordinary moments? Like finding an unexpected path in a garden, you thought you knew completely. Sometimes our deepest knowing comes not in dramatic revelations but in these quiet realizations that keep returning, asking us to pay attention.

Notice what lights you up this week, even if it seems too small to matter. Those tiny sparks of interest or engagement might be showing you something important about where your path wants to lead.

WEEKLY REFLECTION PROMPT 5: WHAT PATTERNS NEED RECOGNITION?

Sometimes the most meaningful patterns in our lives are like background music playing so softly we barely notice it. Yet if we listen carefully, these gentle rhythms often carry messages about what matters most to us. Think of them as the seasons of your inner garden, each with its own wisdom to share.

Sarah encountered an uncomfortable truth: "This week's entries revealed something I've been trying not to see. Three different times, I found myself exhausted after spending time with a certain group of friends. Each time, I told myself it was just bad timing or that I was overtired. But looking at these moments together, I can't ignore the pattern anymore. When I'm with them, I feel like I have to be a brighter, louder version of myself. Writing this makes my chest tight, but maybe recognizing this pattern is the first step toward being more authentic."

James noticed a surprising thread: "Looking back through my entries, I see how often I gravitate toward moments of quiet. Not just physical silence but spaces where I don't have to perform or prove anything. There's a snippet from Monday about feeling peaceful while gardening and another from Thursday about losing track of time while sketching. I always thought I should be more outgoing and more social. But maybe this pattern is showing me something about what actually nourishes me."

Isn't it amazing how our lives keep offering us the same lessons in different wrapping paper? Like a friend who knows we need to hear something important, these patterns persist until we're ready to receive their message. Sometimes what we first see as a problem to fix is actually a doorway into deeper understanding.

This week, look for gentle repetitions in your life. Notice which experiences keep finding you and which feelings return in different situations. Wisdom might be waiting in these recurring themes, not asking for change but simply for recognition.

WEEKLY REFLECTION PROMPT 6: WHAT CONVERSATION AWAITS?

Have you ever noticed how some conversations seem to live in your heart long before they reach your lips? Like a letter you keep drafting in your mind or words that surface in that quiet moment before sleep? This prompt explores those waiting conversations, the ones your heart is slowly preparing to speak.

Sarah discovered layers in her hesitation: "All week, I've been composing letters in my head to my mother. On the surface, I tell myself I'm too busy to call. But these journal entries reveal something deeper. I'm afraid that sharing how different my life choices are from what she hoped for me might disappoint her. Yet something in me knows this conversation needs to happen. Not just about my choices, but about finding my own way of being in the world. The words aren't fully formed yet, but I can feel them gathering."

James found courage in reflection: "Looking back at my entries, I realize I've been rehearsing a conversation with my oldest friend, not about our day-to-day lives but about how our friendship has drifted into comfortable surface chatter. Every time we share a genuine moment of connection, I feel the gap between what we've become and what we could be. I'm nervous about having this discussion, but these entries show me it's becoming more uncomfortable to stay in this shallow water than to wade into deeper truth."

You know how sometimes a conversation feels both necessary and not quite ready? Like fruit that needs just a little more time to ripen? There's wisdom in this waiting. Your journal can be like a gentle gardener, helping these tender words take shape at their own pace. Notice which conversations keep appearing in your entries. They might be with others or even with parts of yourself that are ready to be heard in a new way.

Sometimes just acknowledging these waiting conversations helps us understand what matters most to us right now. Let your journal be a safe place to practice, to find the words that will eventually bridge the spaces between hearts. Trust that when the time is right, you'll know how to begin.

WEEKLY REFLECTION PROMPT 7: WHERE DID VALUES GUIDE CHOICE?

You know those moments when something inside you just knows what's right? Not because anyone told you, but because it aligns with something essential in your heart? Our values often speak to us in these quiet moments of clarity, showing us where the true north lies on our personal compass.

Sarah found wisdom in what felt like a small choice: "Looking back through my entries, a moment from Tuesday keeps glowing. A friend asked me to join a project that everyone said would be 'great exposure.' On paper, it made perfect sense. But something in me kept hesitating. When I finally said no, I felt this unexpected relief. It wasn't about the project, really. It was about honoring this deeper, knowing that my life right now needs more space, not more acclaim. Sometimes saying no to what looks good makes room for what feels right."

James recognized his values by speaking through actions: "My week's entries show this interesting pattern. Three times I chose to sit and really listen to my daughter's stories about school, even though my to-do list was screaming for attention.

In the moment, each choice felt like falling behind. But seeing them together now, I realize these weren't failures of time management. They were moments of being true to what I believe about presence and connection. Maybe efficiency isn't always the highest value."

It's fascinating how our truest values often reveal themselves not in our grand declarations but in these small, daily choices. Like a garden that naturally turns toward the sun, something in us instinctively leans toward what truly matters. These moments might not look impressive from the outside, but they carry a kind of quiet rightness that refreshes our spirit.

This week, notice when your choices leave you feeling that subtle sense of alignment, even if you can't entirely explain why. Your heart might be showing you what you value most.

WEEKLY REFLECTION PROMPT 8: WHAT CHANGE SEEKS EXPRESSION?

Have you ever noticed how real change often begins not with a dramatic decision but with a gentle stirring? Like the first hints of spring appearing in a winter garden, transformation usually whispers before it shouts.

Sarah found herself recognizing subtle signals: "Reading through my entries, I keep finding traces of restlessness. Not the kind that needs immediate action, but something deeper. During quiet moments at home, walking in my neighborhood, and even while making dinner, there's this persistent wondering about a different way of being. Not just doing different things but showing up in life more authentically. The thought both excites and terrifies me. I've built such comfortable patterns, yet something in me knows they might be getting too comfortable."

James noticed change emerging through discomfort: "My reflection this week reveals something I can't ignore anymore. Every time I automatically agree with others just to keep the peace, something in me feels out of tune, like an instrument playing slightly off-key. The moments when I feel most alive are when I dare to share my real thoughts, even if they're different. I worry about disrupting relationships, but I'm beginning to wonder if those relationships might actually deepen with more honesty."

Isn't it interesting how change often feels both inviting and unsettling? Like standing at the edge of a garden path you've never taken before. Part of you wants to stick with the familiar route, while another part knows that new vistas await if you dare to explore.

When change begins stirring in our lives, it often shows up first in these quiet noticings: a growing awareness that something wants to shift, a sense that what used to fit now feels a bit too small. Listen to these gentle whispers. They're often the voice of your own growth calling.

WEEKLY REFLECTION PROMPT 9: WHERE DID JOY BREAK THROUGH?

Sometimes we get so focused on growing and changing that we forget to notice the joy that's already blooming in our lives. It's like having a garden and only seeing the weeds that need pulling, missing the flowers that are already open.

Sarah discovered delight in unexpected corners: "When I look back through my entries, the brightest moments weren't the ones I planned for happiness. They were these small, unscripted times: laughing with my friend when we both got caught in the rain, the quiet satisfaction of making soup from my grandmother's recipe, an impromptu conversation with my neighbor who wandered into sharing childhood dreams. These moments felt true in a way I'm still trying to understand."

James recognized a pattern in his joy: "My entries this week surprised me. The times I felt most alive weren't during scheduled fun activities. They were these simple moments of genuine connection when a conversation went deeper than small talk, when I stopped trying to fix someone's problem and just listened, and when I let myself be fully present without trying to manage the moment. It's almost like joy finds me more easily when I stop chasing it."

You know how sometimes the sweetest moments are the ones you couldn't have planned? Like finding an unexpected bloom in your garden. Joy has a way of surprising us when we relax our grip on how things should be and make room for what naturally unfolds.

This week, notice what brings a smile to your face or a feeling of lightness to your heart. Not because you should, but because these moments of joy might be showing you something important about what makes your life feel rich and real.

WEEKLY REFLECTION PROMPT 10: WHAT TRUTH NEEDS SPACE?

Truth can be like a seed stirring underground. It needs the right conditions to emerge, and sometimes it grows in its own unexpected way. This week's prompt invites you to notice what truths might be ready to break through in your life.

Sarah felt truth emerging through resistance: "Looking at my entries, I notice how often I edit myself in everyday conversations. With family, with friends, even in my private thoughts. It's not just about keeping peace. There's this deeper fear about what might happen if I let people see how differently I think about things. Writing this makes my stomach tight, but I'm starting to recognize how much energy it takes to keep parts of myself hidden. Maybe it's time to let some of my real thoughts see daylight."

James discovered truth in the spaces between: "Going through this week's writing, I see such a gap between my outer and inner life. In public, I focus on appearing confident and together. But my private reflections overflow with questions about life's bigger meanings, wonderings about paths not taken, and doubts about choices I've made. I'm realizing I've become fluent in two languages, the public one and the true one. Carrying both is getting heavier than I expected."

Have you ever noticed how some truths feel like they're waiting for permission to be acknowledged? Like plants reaching toward light, they keep growing despite our attempts to contain them. Sometimes just naming these truths in our journal creates a little more space for them to exist.

This week, notice what truths keep appearing in your reflection, even if they're not fully formed yet. Sometimes understanding grows best when we create conditions for it to emerge naturally, without forcing it into bloom before its time.

WEEKLY REFLECTION PROMPT 11: WHAT GROWTH INVITES YOUR ATTENTION?

We all have those edges in our lives where comfort meets challenge, where what's familiar brushes up against what's possible. These places can feel tender, like newly sprouting plants. But they're often where our most meaningful growth happens.

Sarah recognized the invitation in discomfort: "Reading my entries this week, I notice how defensive I get when someone sees things differently than I do. It happens at family dinners, with friends, and even in casual conversations at the grocery store. I can feel myself building walls, bringing out all my reasons why my way makes sense. What's interesting is that my strongest reactions come when part of me suspects they might have a point. There's something here about being right versus being open that I need to explore, even though everything in me wants to skip these pages and write about something else."

James found his edge in everyday moments: "Looking back through my week, I see how often I stay quiet in conversations that really matter to me. When friends are sharing their deeper thoughts about life, love, and purpose, I find myself nodding along instead of offering my perspective. I tell myself I'm just being a good listener, but these entries show me something else. My silence isn't always about holding space. Sometimes it's about holding back. My growth edge might be learning to trust that my thoughts and feelings deserve room in these conversations too."

You know that feeling when something uncomfortable keeps showing up in your life. It's like a persistent garden plant that returns no matter how often you try to ignore it. Sometimes, these recurring challenges are actually invitations, showing us where we're ready to grow in new ways.

This week, notice what situations consistently stretch you beyond your comfort zone. Where do you feel that mix of resistance and curiosity? That's often where the richest opportunities for growth are waiting.

WEEKLY REFLECTION PROMPT 12: WHAT WISDOM WHISPERS IN QUIET MOMENTS?

Sometimes our deepest knowing speaks most clearly when we're not trying so hard to figure things out. Like how a garden looks different in the gentle light of dawn, wisdom often appears most clearly in those unguarded moments between our busy thoughts.

Sarah found insight in unexpected places: "I always thought wisdom would come from intense study or dramatic revelations. But reading through my entries, I notice how often clarity appears in these simple moments. Watching birds at my kitchen window. Walking around the block without my phone. There's this one moment I keep coming back to. I was waiting for the kettle to boil, not thinking about anything in particular, when I suddenly understood why I keep rushing to fix things for people I love. It wasn't a big lightning bolt moment, but it felt true in a way I can't quite explain."

James discovered understanding in pauses: "The quiet spaces between activities keep showing me something about my relationship with time. Those moments when I'm just sitting in my backyard or driving in silence. My entries are full of insights that arrive when I finally stop trying to figure everything out. Like yesterday, when I was just watching the rain and realized how much of my life I spend preparing for tomorrow instead of living today. These aren't the kind of realizations I can turn into action steps, but they feel important to acknowledge."

Isn't it interesting how wisdom often arrives like a gentle friend, waiting for those moments when we're not trying so hard? When we're just being, without an agenda or goal. Sometimes, our deepest understanding comes not from analyzing or planning but from simply being present enough to notice what we already know.

This week, pay attention to those quiet moments between activities. What whispers of wisdom might be waiting for you there?

WEEKLY REFLECTION PROMPT 13: WHAT WANTS TO SHIFT IN YOUR LIFE?

Life has these fascinating ways of letting us know when we're ready for change. Not always through dramatic events but often through gentle nudges, persistent wonderings, or a quiet sense that something is ready to be different.

Sarah felt movement in familiar patterns: "When I look through my entries, I notice this thought that keeps appearing in different ways. It shows up when I'm going through my usual routines, choosing familiar responses, and staying in comfortable relationships. There's this quiet but persistent question: What if there's another way? Not just of doing things but of being in the world. It's both exciting and terrifying to admit how many parts of my life feel ready for change. Like something in me is outgrowing spaces that used to feel just right."

James recognized shifts in his foundation: "Something interesting appears in my reflections this week. So many things I used to be certain about feel less solid now. My ideas about what makes a good life, what counts as success, and even what happiness means. At first, this uncertainty felt unsettling. Part of me wants to quickly build new certainties to replace the old ones. But another part wonders if maybe learning to live with questions might be more important than having all the answers right now."

You know how sometimes you can feel a shift coming before you know exactly what needs to change? Like sensing the season is about to turn before you see any obvious signs. Our lives have these subtle transition times too, when something in us knows we're ready for something new, even if we can't quite name it yet.

As you reflect this week, notice what parts of your life seem ready for change. Maybe a relationship needs more authenticity, a boundary that needs adjustment, or a dream that needs to be taken more seriously. Trust that these stirrings of change carry their own wisdom about what will emerge in your life next.

BUILDING YOUR WEEKLY PRACTICE

You know how a garden gradually reveals its secrets, revealing different treasures as you spend time with it. Your weekly reflection practice unfolds in much the same way. It's not about forcing insights or checking off prompts from a list. It's about creating a gentle space for understanding to emerge naturally.

Sarah found her practice evolving in unexpected ways: "I used to approach weekly reflection like it was another task to complete, searching for profound insights on schedule. Now I understand it's more like having an ongoing conversation with a trusted friend. Some weeks bring crystal clear understanding, others just quiet questions that need time to unfold. I'm learning that both serve the journey. What matters isn't finding answers but staying curious about what's stirring in my life."

James discovered depth through gentle persistence: " Looking back over several months of weekly reflections, I notice how certain themes keep appearing, like familiar melodies playing in different keys. What starts as a simple observation about feeling restless often opens into deeper questions about what truly matters to me. These patterns aren't problems to solve but invitations to understand myself better. Sometimes the most significant insights come from simply noticing what keeps drawing my attention."

Through regular practice, you develop a more nuanced awareness of your inner landscape. Like a gardener who learns to read subtle changes in their plants, you begin to recognize the quiet signals that point toward growth, the whispers of wisdom that might otherwise go unheard.

MOVING TOWARD DEEPER WATERS

Think about how your understanding of a garden changes through different seasons. Daily tending shows you individual moments of growth. Weekly reflection helps you see patterns in how things grow together. But there's another layer of understanding that comes from an even wider view: seeing how your inner garden changes through entire seasons.

As we prepare to explore monthly reflection, imagine stepping back even further, finding a vantage point that lets you see the larger story your life is trying to tell. Sarah reflects on this natural evolution: "When I first started journaling, I focused only on immediate experiences and reactions. Weekly reflection helped me see patterns in how I respond to life. But something in me feels ready for an even wider view, for understanding the deeper currents that shape my choices and relationships."

James shares his journey toward deeper understanding: "I notice how my weekly reflections often touch on similar themes from different angles. It's like life keeps offering new opportunities to understand old patterns. Monthly reflection feels like a natural next step, a chance to see these recurring themes more clearly and understand their deeper meaning."

This invitation to monthly reflection doesn't replace your daily or weekly practice. Instead, it adds another layer of insight, another perspective from which to witness your life's unfolding. Think of it as expanding your capacity to hold both detail and overview, both immediate experience and larger meaning.

The understanding you've developed through daily and weekly practice and your growing ability to notice patterns and sit with uncertainty create a strong foundation for this deeper work. Like a garden that needs both daily tending and seasonal planning, your inner growth benefits from different rhythms of attention.

As we explore monthly reflection together, carry with you the trust you've developed in your own way of understanding. Remember that each way of reflecting serves its own purpose in your journey. Trust that your capacity for understanding grows naturally as you create space for these varying perspectives.

Let's explore these deeper waters together, carrying the wisdom we've gathered while opening ourselves to even broader horizons of self-discovery.

FOUR
DISCOVERING YOUR INNER LANDSCAPE

D o you know how sometimes you must step back from a garden to see its patterns? Maybe you've had the experience of looking down from a hillside and suddenly noticing how all the different parts of a landscape work together. Monthly reflection offers us this broader view of our inner world, revealing patterns and connections we might miss when we're closer to the ground.

Think of it this way: daily reflection helps us notice individual flowers and leaves, and weekly reflection shows us how different plants grow together. Monthly reflection lets us see the whole garden changing through the seasons. Here, we begin to recognize the deeper rhythms that shape our personal growth.

Sarah discovered this wider perspective quite naturally: "I used to think monthly reflection meant I had to analyze everything that happened in the past four weeks. But one Sunday afternoon, I spread out all my journal entries on my living room floor, made a cup of tea, and just let myself notice what patterns caught my eye. Things that seemed random in the moment started appearing like threads in a tapestry. I realized how often I say yes to things out of fear rather than genuine desire. This wasn't about judging myself. It was about finally seeing a pattern that had been invisible when I was too close to it."

James found his monthly practice evolved with gentleness: "At first, I resisted looking back over a whole month. It felt over-whelming, like too much to hold. Then, I started treating it more like visiting with an old friend. I'd take my journal to this quiet café I love, order my favorite coffee, and just spend time with my own story. Sometimes, I notice practical things, like how my energy flows through the month. Other times, I discover deeper patterns, like how my need for certainty shows up in so many different disguises. The key was learning to look with curiosity instead of criticism."

Monthly reflection isn't about analyzing everything or finding things to fix. It's more like giving yourself the gift of a broader perspective. Imagine sitting with a dear friend who knows you well, looking back over your journey with warmth and under-standing. This kind of reflection helps you recognize the larger stories playing out in your life, the deeper currents that shape your choices and relationships.

Let's explore some prompts that can help us discover these broader patterns. Remember, there's no need to use every prompt every month. Think of them as gentle invitations, different windows through which to view your inner land-scape. Trust that the patterns that need your attention will naturally draw your eye.

MONTHLY DEEP DIVE PROMPT 1: WHAT HIDDEN PATTERNS SHAPED YOUR CHOICES?

Do you know those moments when you suddenly notice something that's been there all along? Maybe it's realizing your favorite walking path always takes you past gardens or noticing you consistently choose the same corner of a café. Our choices often follow patterns we don't see until we step back far enough to notice them.

Sarah noticed a surprising thread: "Looking back through a month of entries, something interesting emerged. Whenever I faced uncertainty, whether choosing weekend plans or joining a new community group, I defaulted to what felt safe rather than what quietly called to my heart. In each moment, it just felt like making a sensible choice. But seeing them all together, I recognized an old pattern. This wasn't about being practical. It was about an old belief that fitting in matters more than following my own star.

What caught my attention was how incomplete these 'safe' choices left me feeling—like wearing clothes that fit perfectly but aren't quite your style. Understanding this pattern helps me recognize why some decisions, even when they make perfect sense on paper, leave me feeling disconnected.

James discovered his own pattern through reflection: "Something surprising showed up when I looked back over this month's entries. I keep putting everyone else's growth ahead of my own. When friends need support, I'm there in a heartbeat. When the family needs help working through challenges, I drop everything. These feel like natural choices in the moment. But seeing them together, I realize I've been using others' needs to avoid facing my own questions about where

I'm headed. It's not that supporting others is wrong. I've been using it to hide from my own path."

Isn't it fascinating how our choices whisper stories about what we believe? Like footprints in a garden, they leave traces of our deeper truths. Sometimes, these patterns serve us beautifully, guiding us toward what truly matters. Other times, they reveal old beliefs that might be ready for gentle questioning.

As you look back over your month, notice what choices keep appearing. Maybe you'll see patterns in the quiet moments when you instinctively reach for certain comforts, the social situations where you find yourself playing familiar roles, the decisions that leave you feeling either energized or depleted, and the dreams you consistently postpone "until later."

Remember, noticing patterns isn't about judging them right or wrong. It's more like understanding the layout of your inner garden. Some patterns might be like well-worn paths that still serve you well. Others might be showing you where new paths want to emerge.

Take your time with this reflection. Maybe spread out your journal entries somewhere comfortable, make yourself a favorite drink, and just notice what catches your attention. Trust that the patterns that matter most will naturally draw your eye, like sunlight highlighting certain flowers in a garden.

MONTHLY DEEP DIVE PROMPT 2: WHEN DID YOU FEEL MOST NATURALLY YOURSELF?

Have you ever noticed how some moments just feel right? Like finding that perfect spot in the sun where you can fully relax. This prompt invites us to see those times when we felt most at home in our own skin when we weren't trying to be anything other than who we were.

Sarah discovered her authentic moments in unexpected places: "Looking back through my month, I noticed something surprising. My most authentic self showed up strongly in those early morning hours before anyone else was awake. It was just me, my coffee, and the quiet. There were no expectations to meet and no roles to fill. I wrote about things I usually keep hidden, dreaming about possibilities I typically dismiss as impractical. Even my body felt different—more relaxed, more at home.

What caught my attention was how this feeling appeared during an impromptu conversation with my neighbor. We started talking about our childhood dreams, and suddenly, I found myself sharing thoughts I usually keep to myself. Something about that unplanned moment let me drop the usual social mask and just be real."

James recognized his authentic self in unscripted moments: "Reading through my entries, I noticed how alive I felt during those weekend mornings when I let myself follow whatever naturally interests me. Sometimes, that meant getting lost in a book; other times, working in my garden or calling an old friend. These weren't productive moments by usual standards, but they felt deeply true. Like I was following an inner compass instead of an external should."

It's fascinating how authenticity often appears when we're not trying to make it happen, like wildflowers that bloom best when we don't overmanage them. These moments of feeling ourselves naturally offer important clues about what nourishes our spirit.

As you reflect on your month, consider those times when you felt most at ease, most alive, and most genuinely yourself. Maybe these were quiet moments alone, or they appeared in unexpected connections with others. Trust that these glimpses of your authentic self have something valuable to tell you about what helps you thrive.

MONTHLY DEEP DIVE PROMPT 3: WHAT MASKS DID YOU WEAR?

Think about how different plants in a garden might need different kinds of protection. Some need shade from the harsh sun; others need support to climb. As humans, we also develop various ways of protecting ourselves and the masks we wear in different situations. This month, let's gently explore these masks with curiosity rather than judgment.

Sarah recognized familiar costumes: "When I noticed how I moved through this month, I saw the different roles I slipped into almost automatically. I became the peacemaker at family dinners, smoothing tensions before they could surface. With certain friends, I'm the one who keeps things light and fun, carefully steering away from deeper waters. Even alone, I caught myself playing the role of someone who has it all figured out.

But there were these early morning moments before I put on any of these masks when I glimpsed a different self—someone who feels uncertain but also more accurate and has questions instead of answers. I'm starting to wonder: "Who am I when no one needs anything from me?"

James discovered patterns in his protection: "This month showed me how I wear different masks in different relation-ships. There's the always-patient friend, the perpetually strong one who never needs support, the person who has a clear direction in life. Looking at these masks together, I realize they all share a common thread. They're all ways of keeping people at a safe distance from my own vulnerability. The real question isn't whether these masks are good or bad. It's whether they're still serving me or if some of them are ready to be set aside."

Our masks often develop for good reasons. They help us navigate social waters and protect tender parts of ourselves. But sometimes, like plants that have outgrown their supports, we might be ready for more freedom and authenticity in how we show up.

Notice which masks feel light and helpful, like a sun hat on a bright day, and which might grow heavy. There's no rush to change anything. Awareness of these patterns opens the door for more conscious choices about when and how we want to protect ourselves.

MONTHLY DEEP DIVE PROMPT 4: WHAT DO YOUR BOUNDARIES TELL YOU ABOUT YOUR NEEDS?

Just as a garden needs thoughtful borders to thrive, our lives need boundaries that protect what's precious to us. But sometimes, what we think about setting boundaries is really about discovering our deeper needs. Let's explore what your boundary patterns might be trying to tell you.

Sarah's reflection revealed surprising insights: "Looking back over this month, I noticed my need for quiet time isn't just about being introverted. It's about creating a space where my creativity can unfold without judgment. I wasn't just setting a boundary whenever I protected my morning writing time or said no to evening plans. I was honoring this deep need for self-expression that I'm only beginning to understand.

These aren't just preferences; they're essential requirements for my well-being. Like a plant that needs specific conditions to flower, I'm learning that my spirit needs certain kinds of space to truly bloom."

James found wisdom in his limits: "Through this month's entries, I see how my boundaries often felt like apologies. 'Sorry, I can't make it.' 'Sorry, I need time to think about that.' But when I look closer, I see that these weren't limitations to feel bad about. They were expressions of self-respect, ways of saying my needs matter too. Understanding this helps me set boundaries with more confidence, knowing they're not walls that keep people out but garden borders that help good things grow."

As you look back over your month, notice your yeses and nos. What do they tell you about what matters most to you? Where do you naturally create firm boundaries, and where do you find them more challenging to maintain? Often, our clearest boundaries protect what we value most deeply.

MONTHLY DEEP DIVE PROMPT 5: WHICH OLD STORIES GOT CHALLENGED?

We all carry stories about who we are, like well-worn paths through a familiar garden. But sometimes, life presents experiences that make us question these old narratives. This month, let's notice which of your stories might be ready for gentle revision.

Sarah watched an old story shift: "I've always told myself I'm not naturally creative, that I'm more of a practical person. But this month challenged that belief in unexpected ways. When our neighborhood faced a problem with local traffic, I developed innovative solutions that brought the community together. My journal entries show my surprise at this side of myself emerging.

Seeing this old story start to unravel helps me recognize how often I've used 'I'm not creative' as a reason to stay in comfortable routines rather than explore new possibilities."

James recognized a familiar narrative changing: "The story I've always told myself is that I need everything planned out to feel secure. But looking through this month's experiences, I notice how often my best moments came from following unexpected opportunities. This challenges my whole identity as someone who always knows what's next. Maybe there's a different kind of security in trusting life's unplanned invitations."

These old stories often protected us in some way, like a fence around a young plant. But sometimes, like that same plant growing stronger, we might be ready for more space and more possibilities. Watch for moments this month when reality didn't match your usual narrative about yourself. These mismatches often point toward new growth trying to emerge.

MONTHLY DEEP DIVE PROMPT 6: HOW DID YOUR VALUES GUIDE YOUR PATH?

Sometimes, our most authentic values speak to us in whispers. Not through the big declarations we make about what matters but through those quiet moments when something inside us knows what feels right. Let's explore how your values might have quietly guided you this month.

Sarah discovered her values by speaking through small choices: "Looking back through my entries, I noticed how authenticity kept showing up as a gentle compass. At this moment, everyone was excited about a trendy new social group, and something in me quietly said, 'Not for me.' At the time, I worried I was being antisocial. But seeing it now, I realize I was honoring my need for genuine connection over just being part of the crowd.

What interests me is how clear these values feel when I look back, even though they weren't obvious in the moment. My heart knows what matters before my mind catches up."

James recognized his values in unexpected places: "This month showed me how deeply I value creating space for others to be themselves, not in any dramatic way, but in small moments. For example, when my brother shared something vulnerable, I naturally protected that moment from interruption. When a friend was exploring a new interest, I felt this surge of joy in witnessing their excitement. These weren't conscious decisions, but my values quietly showed the way."

It's incredible how our values often reveal themselves, not in our planned actions but in these natural responses, such as plants naturally turning toward sunlight. Looking back over time, we can see the invisible compass guiding our choices.

What values have been quietly shaping your path this month? Maybe you'll notice them in the most right moments or when something inside you said "no" even when you couldn't explain why.

MONTHLY DEEP DIVE PROMPT 7: WHAT NATURALLY DREW YOUR ENERGY?

Think about how specific activities make you lose track of time, like being so absorbed in tending a beautiful garden that afternoon slips into the evening without you noticing. These moments of natural engagement often have something important to tell us about what truly energizes our spirit.

Sarah found a pattern in her enthusiasm: "Reading through my month, I noticed how my energy naturally rises whenever I'm helping someone see a situation in a new way, not by giving advice but by asking questions that open up different perspectives. In these conversations, I completely lose track of time. It's not about being helpful. Something about exploring possibilities with another person makes me feel fully alive.

What catches my attention is how different this feels from what I thought I 'should' be focusing on. It's like discovering your garden's best flowers are the ones that planted themselves."

James recognized his natural pull: "This month showed me something surprising about my energy. It peaks in those unplanned moments of deep conversation with old friends or new acquaintances. I feel this incredible aliveness when someone shares something real about their life, and we drop below the surface of small talk. It's teaching me something about what truly matters to me, beyond what I thought I should care about."

Notice what activities or moments naturally light you up. Where does time seem to flow differently? What conversations or activities leave you feeling more energized than when you began? Sometimes, our deepest callings whisper through these moments of natural engagement.

MONTHLY DEEP DIVE PROMPT 8: HOW DID YOUR BODY SHARE ITS WISDOM?

Our bodies often know things before our minds catch up, like feeling the weather about to change before seeing any clouds. This month, let's listen to the quiet wisdom your body has been trying to share.

Sarah noticed physical patterns speaking: "When I look back, I see how my body was sending me messages I initially missed. Those headaches weren't just about needing more water. They appeared every time I agreed to something that didn't feel quite right. My shoulders would tighten before I even consciously recognized the discomfort. My body was saying 'pay attention' long before my mind understood why.

The most interesting part was noticing how my energy naturally flows through the day. There are times when creativity comes easily and times when my body asks for rest. Learning to work with these rhythms instead of fighting them has been surprisingly robust."

James discovered wisdom in physical signals: "My body had been trying to tell me something important. That tension in my shoulders wasn't just about poor posture. It showed up specifically when I was holding back from expressing something true. Once I started paying attention to this pattern, I realized my body was offering guidance about authenticity. It's like having an inner compass I'd been ignoring."

If we learn to listen, our bodies hold such deep wisdom. Notice what physical sensations have been recurring this month. What situations create tension? When does your body feel most at ease? These physical patterns often point toward essential truths about what we need.

MONTHLY DEEP DIVE PROMPT 9: WHICH PARTS OF YOURSELF STAYED HIDDEN?

We all have aspects of ourselves we tend to keep in the shadows, like parts of a garden we hesitate to show visitors. Let's gently explore what parts of yourself might be asking for more light and air this month.

Sarah recognized familiar hiding places: "Looking back, I notice how often I tuck away my more emotional side, especially in friendships. If someone asks how I'm doing, I share the practical details but rarely the feelings underneath. Even in my closest relationships, I catch myself editing out the messy, uncertain parts of my experience. It's not just about privacy. This more profound fear is that being fully seen might somehow be too much.

"What's interesting is realizing how exhausting it is to conceal parts of myself. Like trying to prevent certain flowers from blooming in a garden, it requires so much energy to uphold these careful boundaries."

James found patterns in his protective habits: "This month showed me how I often hide my struggles while encouraging others to be open about theirs. It's this strange contradiction. I believe deeply in the value of vulnerability, yet I keep my doubts and questions carefully tucked away. Seeing this pattern helps me understand where I might need to practice what I believe about the beauty of being human and imperfect."

Sometimes, the parts we hide carry our deepest gifts. Not everything must be shared, but noticing what we keep hidden often reveals important truths about our fears and longings.

MONTHLY DEEP DIVE PROMPT 10: WHEN DID LIFE FEEL MOST REAL?

Think about those moments when time seems to slow down, and you feel completely present, like when you're fully absorbed in watching a sunset or deeply engaged in a heartfelt conversation. These moments of feeling fully alive often have something important to tell us about what matters most.

Sarah found aliveness in unexpected places: "The times I felt most real this month weren't the significant events or achievements. They were these simple, unplanned moments: walking in the rain and feeling utterly present with the sensation of water on my skin; a long conversation with my sister where we finally moved past our usual roles and spoke from our hearts; sitting in my garden early one morning and feeling perfectly content just being there.

These moments had something in common. They all happened when I wasn't trying to be anything in particular. Just fully present with whatever was unfolding."

James discovered vitality in genuine connection: "Reading through my entries, I notice how alive I felt during completely ordinary moments that somehow became extraordinary. Like when a casual chat with a neighbor turned into a deep discussion about dreams, we'd almost forgotten. Or that afternoon I spent simply watching birds in my backyard. Something about dropping our usual rushing and being fully present makes life feel more real."

Notice what moments this month felt most authentic to you. When did time seem to slow down? When did you feel most present and alive? These experiences often point us toward what truly nourishes our spirit.

MONTHLY DEEP DIVE PROMPT 11: WHAT MADE YOU STEP BACK?

Do you know those moments when something inside you quietly says, "Not yet," or "Maybe this needs a different approach?" This kind of resistance often carries wisdom, like when your garden shows you it needs something different from what you planned to give it.

Sarah found herself exploring unexpected hesitation: "Looking through my month, I noticed how public recognition often made me want to disappear. When friends wanted to celebrate my art show, part of me appreciated their enthusiasm, but another part felt oddly exposed. It wasn't about being humble. This resistance tried to tell me something about my relationship with being seen.

The interesting part was realizing this wasn't about recognition itself. It connected to the old story that staying under the radar means staying safe. Seeing this pattern helps me distinguish between genuine modesty and old fears asking to be gentled."

James discovered layers in his resistance: "All month, I found myself pulling back from group gatherings I usually enjoy. At first, I thought I was just being antisocial. But when I sat with this feeling, I realized my spirit was asking for something different—not isolation but a more authentic way of connecting. Those moments of resistance were actually inviting me toward deeper, more genuine relationships."

Sometimes, what looks like resistance is wisdom in disguise. Notice what consistently makes you pause or step back this month. Rather than pushing through, try getting curious about what these moments might be trying to tell you.

MONTHLY DEEP DIVE PROMPT 12: HOW DID YOUR RELATIONSHIPS MIRROR YOU?

It's fascinating how our relationships often reflect parts of ourselves we might not otherwise see, like catching glimpses of your reflection in a still pond. This month, let's explore what your interactions might be showing you about yourself.

Sarah recognized herself in her reactions: "I noticed how strongly I reacted to my friend's perfectionism, how it bothered me to watch her constantly revise her work. Then, one evening, writing in my journal, it hit me. I was seeing my own inner critic reflected in her actions. My frustration wasn't really about her. It was showing me something about my own relationship with getting things right.

This shifted everything. Each challenging interaction became a window into better understanding myself. Even the things that irritate me most in others started looking more like invitations to self-awareness."

James found wisdom in patterns: "This month showed me something interesting about how I respond to people seeking constant reassurance. I realized my impatience wasn't about them. It was mirroring my struggle with self-trust. Each time I felt that frustration rise, it pointed to places where I still questioned my knowing."

Isn't it amazing how the things that trigger us strongest in others often connect to parts of ourselves asking for attention? Like a garden showing you what it needs through what naturally thrives or struggles, our relationships can reveal essential truths about our inner landscape.

MONTHLY DEEP DIVE PROMPT 13: WHAT SYMBOLS KEPT APPEARING?

Sometimes, our deeper wisdom speaks to us through images and symbols, like recurring themes in a dream or specific patterns that keep catching our eye. Let's notice what images or symbols might have been trying to get your attention this month.

Sarah watched a pattern emerge: "The image of locked doors kept showing up, both in my dreams and my waking life. I'd notice it in books I read, conversations with friends, and even in random street art. At first, I thought it was a coincidence. But sitting with this symbol, I started wondering if it was showing me something about opportunities I might be closing myself off from.

What's fascinating is how these symbols often point to truths we're almost ready to recognize. Like they're helping us understand something important just slightly before we're ready to see it directly."

James found meaning in recurring signs: "Birds kept appearing in my awareness. Not just actual birds but references to them in conversations, songs, and even ads that caught my eye. When I finally paid attention to this pattern, I realized it was speaking to something in me that longed for more freedom, more space to explore life without so many self-imposed restrictions."

Notice what images or symbols keep drawing your attention this month. Certain animals, colors, or elements in nature may appear repeatedly. These patterns often carry messages from our deeper knowing.

MONTHLY DEEP DIVE PROMPT 14: WHERE DID YOU SEEK OUTSIDE APPROVAL?

We all have moments when we look outside ourselves for confirmation that we're on the right path. It's natural, like checking a map during a journey. But sometimes, these moments can show us where we might need to strengthen our inner compass.

Sarah noticed a subtle pattern: "Looking back through my entries, I see how often I ran decisions past others before trusting my knowing. Even small choices, like what to do with a free afternoon, somehow felt safer if someone else validated them. This wasn't about getting input. It was about looking for permission to trust my own preferences.

The interesting part was noticing how different I felt on the rare occasions when I simply moved forward with what felt right to me. This quiet confidence had nothing to do with whether others approved."

James found insight in his hesitation: "This month showed me how much energy I spend imagining others' reactions before making choices. It's subtle. I am not asking directly for approval, but I constantly adjust my actions based on what I think others might think or feel. Seeing this pattern helps me recognize when I need to check back in with my knowing."

Notice when you find yourself seeking external validation this month. Not to judge it but to understand what parts of yourself might be asking for more trust and confidence.

MONTHLY DEEP DIVE PROMPT 15: WHAT TRUTH BECAME CLEARER?

Sometimes, understanding emerges slowly, like a photograph gradually developing or a garden revealing its natural patterns over time. This month, let's notice what truths have quietly become clearer in your life.

Sarah discovered an emerging clarity: "When I look over my entries, I see how much I value creative freedom, even though I often choose more structured approaches. It's like this artist in me keeps peeking out, wanting more space to play and explore. I notice how alive I feel when I follow creative impulses, yet how quickly I can abandon them for more 'practical' choices.

This growing clarity about my need for creative expression helps me understand my joy and restlessness. It's showing me something important about what my spirit needs to thrive."

James recognized a deepening truth: "This month revealed something fundamental about what matters most to me. Beyond achievements or recognition, a genuine human connection makes me feel most alive. While I've always known I valued relationships, seeing this theme appear repeatedly in my entries helped me understand it's not just important. It's essential to who I am."

What truths have been gradually revealing themselves in your life? Sometimes, these revelations come not in dramatic moments but in quiet realizations that grow clearer over time, like understanding the natural rhythm of your garden.

NURTURING YOUR MONTHLY PRACTICE

Do you know how a garden reveals different secrets depending on when you visit? The early morning shows you one kind of beauty, twilight another, and then there's that special clarity from watching it change throughout the seasons. Monthly reflection offers a wider view of our inner landscape, helping us recognize the deeper rhythms that shape our growth.

Sarah discovered this broader perspective brought unexpected gifts: "At first, I worried that looking back over an entire month would feel overwhelming. But it's actually become one of my favorite practices. It's like having a long, honest conversation with myself. Some months bring crystal-clear insights, while others just help me notice questions I need to sit with longer. I'm learning that both kinds of understanding matter.

What surprised me was how this monthly pause started changing my daily experience. Where I used to rush past uncomfortable moments, I now find myself curious about them. That awkward conversation with my sister last week became an invitation to understand my patterns around family dynamics rather than just a moment to survive. Having a wider lens helps me see each moment more clearly."

James found his practice deepening naturally: "Monthly reflection has become like checking in with an old friend who really knows me. I take my journal to this quiet café I love, order my favorite coffee, and just spend time with my own story. Sometimes, I notice practical things, like how my energy moves in cycles. Other times, I discover deeper patterns, like how certain old beliefs keep shaping my choices. The key was learning to look with curiosity instead of criticism.

What touches me most is how this practice has helped me be gentler with myself. Seeing patterns over time helps me understand that growth isn't always linear. Some insights need time to ripen, like fruit that shouldn't be rushed to sweeten."

MOVING TOWARD LIFE'S LIVING MOMENTS

As we explore situational prompts, imagine how your growing self-awareness can illuminate those key moments when life asks something special of you. The patterns you've recognized through monthly reflection become like trusted guides, helping you navigate life's challenges and opportunities with more wisdom and grace.

Think of it this way:

Daily journaling helps you notice the weather of your inner world.

Weekly reflection shows you the patterns in that weather.

Monthly reflection reveals the seasons of your soul.

Now, we will explore how all this understanding can serve you in those crucial moments when life presents you with particular challenges or opportunities.

These situations might be transitions you see coming, like moving to a new city or choosing to deepen a relationship. Or they might be unexpected moments that catch you by surprise, like a sudden conflict or an unexpected chance to follow a dream. Either way, the self-awareness you've developed through regular reflection becomes your compass, helping you find your way through new territory.

Sarah reflects on this evolution: "Understanding my patterns helps me show up differently in important moments. Instead of just reacting to old habits, I can pause and remember what I've learned about myself. It doesn't mean I always get it right, but I have more available choices about how to respond."

James shares a similar discovery: "Monthly reflection showed me my tendency to step back when things get uncertain. When I notice that happening, I can ask myself what's really needed here. Sometimes, stepping back is wise. Other times, it's just an old pattern that needs gentle challenge. Having this bigger perspective helps me choose more consciously."

Remember everything you've learned about your inner landscape as we explore situational prompts. Self-awareness isn't about getting somewhere or fixing anything. It's about bringing more consciousness and compassion to your life's unfolding journey.

Let's discover together how the wisdom you've gathered can illuminate those key moments when life invites you to grow in new ways. Turn the page when you're ready to explore how self-awareness can transform the way you meet life's unique situations.

FIVE
MEETING LIFE'S KEY MOMENTS WITH WISDOM

You know those moments in life that seem to ask something special of you? Maybe it's when an old pattern suddenly becomes clear, or your heart whispers something needs to change. Perhaps it's in those quiet instances when joy feels unexpectedly complicated, or your body tries to tell you something your mind hasn't entirely caught up to.

Think of situational prompts as trusted friends who understand these moments. They are not like your daily journal practice, which helps you notice the regular rhythms of your inner weather, your weekly reflection, which shows you patterns, or even your monthly deep dives, which reveal entire seasons of growth. These prompts are more like having a wise companion with you when life presents one of those moments that feels particularly meaningful or challenging.

Sarah discovered these prompts during an unexpected afternoon of insight: "I was sitting in my favorite corner of the garden, feeling oddly uncomfortable about some recent praise I'd received. Usually, I'd push past that feeling and tell myself I was being silly. But I remembered this prompt about our relationship with recognition. Instead of brushing off my discomfort, I got curious about it. The prompt helped me explore what was really happening. It wasn't about the praise at all. It was about an old story I carried about staying safe by staying small. Understanding this changed not just that moment but how I meet similar moments now."

James found these prompts particularly helpful during times of change: "What I love about these prompts is how they meet you exactly where you are. One morning, I noticed this familiar anxiety creeping in about some changes in my life. Instead of fighting or getting lost in it, I turned to the prompt about how change affects us. It was like having a friend gently ask just the right questions. Not to fix anything but to help me understand what was really moving through me. These prompts have become trusted companions for all those moments when life feels rich or challenging."

Think of your garden again. Your daily practice helps you tend to the regular needs of your plants. Weekly reflection shows you how different parts of the garden work together. Monthly deep dives reveal the larger cycles of growth and change. But sometimes, specific situations arise. Maybe a particular plant isn't thriving, an unexpected frost threatens, or a new flower suddenly blooms in a surprising place. These are the moments when you need focused attention and specific wisdom.

These situational prompts offer exactly that kind of focused wisdom. They're designed to help you meet life's key moments with greater understanding and care. Whether you're exploring boundaries, examining old patterns, understanding your relationship with rest or recognition, or navigating any of life's meaningful moments, these prompts offer gentle guidance and thoughtful questions.

Sarah reflects on how these prompts changed her relationship with challenging moments: "I used to think self-reflection was just about regular practice. But life doesn't always wait for your scheduled journal time. Sometimes, you need wisdom right in the moment. These prompts have taught me that every situation, even the uncomfortable ones, carries gifts of understanding if we know how to unwrap them."

James adds, "What surprised me most was how these prompts helped me recognize patterns I might have missed otherwise. When something triggers a strong reaction, I notice myself pulling back from the connection or even when inspiration suddenly strikes, and these prompts help me understand what's happening beneath the surface. They're like having a collection of wise questions always ready when you needed."

As we explore these prompts, remember that they are not about finding quick answers or fixing anything. They are about developing a deeper understanding of yourself through life's many meaningful moments. Think of them as trusted companions for your journey, ready to help you explore whatever arises with curiosity and care.

SIX

A GUIDE TO SITUATIONAL PROMPTS

Y ou know those moments in life that seem to ask for our attention? Times when emotions catch us by surprise, when old patterns surface, or when something shifts in a relationship? These prompts are like trusted friends ready to help you explore those meaningful moments more deeply.

Each prompt begins with "When" because they're designed to meet you in specific situations as they arise. Think of them as invitations to pause and notice what's really happening, both on the surface and in the quiet depths of your experience.

As you write to these prompts, you might consider:

- What drew your attention to this particular moment?
- What feelings, sensations, or thoughts are present?
- What patterns or themes might be revealing themselves?
- What wisdom is waiting to be discovered?

Some reflections might flow quickly, filling pages with sudden insight. Others might need time to unfold like a garden gradually revealing its secrets. Trust that whatever emerges is exactly what needs to be examined right now. There's no right way to respond, only your authentic exploration of the moment.

Let these prompts be gentle guides for understanding life's meaningful moments. Use them whenever a situation calls for deeper reflection, knowing each exploration adds to your self-understanding.

Here are prompts to help you explore your life. Look at when feelings pop up. See times you felt proud of yourself. Think about close bonds with others. Pay attention to what your body tells you. Notice how you have changed and grown.

Be true to who you are. Let your creativity flow freely. Know your own worth. Dream about what could be. Listen to your gut feelings. Learn from your friends and family. See how far you've come. Think about tough times you got through. Notice life's ups and downs. Find joy in small things.

Remember big choices you made. Learn from what you've been through. Give help and take help. Find out who you are in quiet times. Feel like you belong. Find your pace in life. Enjoy the ride.

These prompts help you look at feelings, worth, bonds, body cues, growth, truth, art, praise, dreams, gut feels, ties with others, your path, hard times, life cycles, joy, choices, lessons, give and take, quiet thoughts, fitting in, your rhythm, and your journey.

WHEN EMOTIONS SURFACE

Sometimes, our feelings catch us off guard, like unexpected blooms in our garden. These moments often carry important messages about what matters to us and what needs our attention.

Prompt 1: When Emotions Surprise You. Those times when your feelings seem bigger than the moment. Like when a casual comment stirs unexpected anger or joy appears in an unlikely place. These reactions often point to deeper truths that want to be known.

Prompt 2: When Your 'No' Feels Hard. Setting boundaries can bring up complicated feelings. It's not just about saying no. It's about understanding your relationship with limits, worth, and the courage to honor your own needs.

Prompt 3: When Old Patterns Surface. These familiar dances with life keep returning, like catching yourself preparing too much for something simple or noticing how you withdraw in certain situations. These patterns often carry wisdom about what shaped us and what might be ready to change.

RECOGNIZING WORTH AND VALUE

Our relationship with recognition and achievement often reveals deeper truths about how we value ourselves. These prompts help us gently explore those tender territories.

Prompt 4: When Praise Makes You Uncomfortable. Describe those surprising moments when recognition brings discomfort rather than joy. Sometimes, our reaction to praise reveals old stories about worthiness and visibility that need gentle attention.

Prompt 5: When Achievements Feel Empty. The times when reaching a goal leaves you feeling strangely hollow. These moments often invite us to explore what truly matters to us beyond external markers of success.

Prompt 6: When Comparison Steals Joy. Those times when looking at others' paths make you question your own. This prompt helps you understand what comparison might be trying to tell you about your own dreams and needs.

UNDERSTANDING CONNECTION

Like plants that grow differently in different companions, our relationships reveal important truths about ourselves.

Prompt 7: When Connection Feels Scary. The moments when deepening relationships bring up unexpected fears. These feelings often carry wisdom about old hurts and new possibilities for genuine connection.

Prompt 8: When Solitude Calls. When your spirit asks for quiet. This isn't just about being alone; it's about understanding your need for inner connection and renewal.

Prompt 9: When Others' Needs Feel Too Heavy. This prompt explores the moments when caring for others overshadows your own needs. It helps you balance compassion and self-care.

LISTENING TO BODY WISDOM

Our bodies carry deep knowing, like a garden that responds to changes in weather before we notice them consciously. These prompts help us understand the physical wisdom we often overlook.

Prompt 10: When Your Body Says No. Those moments when physical signals try to get your attention. The headaches that appear in certain situations, and the tension that comes with specific choices. Our bodies often understand our needs before our minds catch up.

Prompt 11: When Energy Drains. Describe the times when certain situations or interactions leave you feeling depleted. This isn't just about being tired. It's about recognizing what nourishes your spirit and what asks too much.

Prompt 12: When Rest Feels Wrong. This prompt addresses those uncomfortable moments when taking a break brings up guilt or anxiety. It helps you explore your relationship with rest and productivity and understand what true renewal means for you.

GROWTH AND TRANSFORMATION

Just as gardens go through natural cycles of growth and change, our inner landscapes constantly evolve. These prompts help us navigate those transformative moments.

Prompt 13: When Change Feels Threatening. The times when possibility and fear dance together. When something in you knows it's time to grow, another part wants to hold onto the familiar. This prompt helps you understand both the resistance and the invitation.

Prompt 14: When Your Past Self Visits. These are the moments when old versions of yourself appear, maybe in how you react to certain situations or in memories that suddenly feel present. These visits often carry wisdom about how far you've come and what still needs attention.

Prompt 15: When Growth Requires Release. The times when moving forward means letting go of something familiar. Like a plant outgrowing its pot, sometimes growth asks us to release old containers that once kept us safe.

INNER TRUTH AND AUTHENTICITY

Sometimes, life presents moments that ask us to choose between comfort and truth. These prompts help us navigate those times when authenticity calls.

Prompt 16: When Authenticity Feels Risky. This prompt explores those moments when being real feels vulnerable— when something in you wants to speak up, but old habits of hiding feel safer. It helps you explore what makes truth-telling feel dangerous and what wants to be expressed.

Prompt 17: When Your Inner Voice Whispers. These are the times when your deeper knowing tries to get your attention, maybe through quiet hunches, persistent thoughts, or dreams that keep returning. This prompt helps you listen to your own wisdom more clearly.

Prompt 18: When Values Need Voice. This prompt is for situations when something important feels at stake. While compromise might be easier, something in you knows it's time to stand up for what matters. It helps you understand and honor your core values.

CREATIVITY AND NATURAL EXPRESSION

Sometimes, our creative spirit asks for attention in unexpected ways. Like wildflowers pushing through garden paths, our natural gifts often seek expression in their timing.

Prompt 19: When Creativity Demands Space. Those restless moments when something in you needs to be created. Maybe it shows up as an unexplained urge to try something new or a familiar activity suddenly feeling too small. This prompt helps you understand what part of your creative spirit asks to bloom.

Prompt 20: When Inspiration Visits. These are moments when ideas or possibilities unexpectedly light you up. These moments of natural enthusiasm often reveal what truly energizes your spirit and show you where your authentic gifts want to flow.

Prompt 21: When Expression Feels Risky. This prompt is for those times when sharing your creative voice brings up butterflies. It is when something in you wants to be expressed, but old doubts whisper caution. This prompt helps you explore what makes sharing feel vulnerable and what wants to be born anyway.

WORTH AND RECOGNITION

Our relationship with personal value often shows itself in subtle ways, like how different plants respond uniquely to the same sunlight.

Prompt 22: When Help is Hard to Accept. There are moments when receiving support feels uncomfortable. This isn't just about independence. It's about understanding your relationship with worthiness and connection.

Prompt 23: When the Inner Critic Gets Loud. This prompt is for those times when self-judgment takes over. When that critical inner voice starts listing all the reasons why you're not enough, it helps you understand what triggers harsh self-talk and what gentler wisdom might be waiting underneath.

Prompt 24: When Success Feels Scary. The surprising moments when achieving something brings up anxiety instead of celebration. Like a plant that's outgrown its familiar pot, sometimes success asks us to expand in uncertain or unexpected ways.

DREAMS AND GENTLE POSSIBILITIES

Some of our deepest truths manifest as quiet longings or persistent wonderings, like seeds waiting for the right season to sprout.

Prompt 25: When Dreams Feel Foolish. Those times when your heart's desires seem impractical or too big. When something in you yearns for more, but another part says it's unrealistic. This prompt helps you explore what your dreams might be telling you about your path.

Prompt 26: When Possibility Whispers. The quiet moments when you glimpse different ways your life could unfold. Maybe through unexpected interests, persistent daydreams, or paths that keep drawing your attention. This prompt helps you listen to these gentle invitations.

Prompt 27: When Old Dreams Resurface. Those times when forgotten aspirations suddenly reappear. Like perennial plants returning in spring, some dreams keep coming back because they carry important truths about who you are.

LISTENING TO INNER WISDOM

Sometimes, our deepest knowing speaks in whispers, like the subtle signs telling a gardener a plant needs something different. These prompts help us tune into our natural wisdom.

Prompt 28: When Your Intuition Nudges. Those quiet moments when something in you just knows. Maybe it's a gentle feeling about a situation or a persistent thought that keeps returning. This prompt helps you trust those subtle signals from your inner wisdom.

Prompt 29: When Silence Reveals Truth. The times when stepping back from noise brings clarity. Like how a garden looks different in the early morning light, sometimes our truths become clearer in quiet moments.

Prompt 30: When Your Heart Knows First. Those instances when your emotional wisdom runs ahead of your logical mind. When something feels deeply right or wrong before you can explain why, this prompt helps you honor your heart's intelligence.

RELATIONSHIPS AND GROWING EDGES

Our connections with others often reveal important truths about ourselves, like how certain plants disclose the nature of the soil they grow in.

Prompt 31: When Boundaries Need Tending. Describe those moments when you sense your limits being stretched. Maybe it's in how much you give, what you allow, or where you draw your lines. This prompt helps you understand and honor your needs for a healthy space.

Prompt 32: When Others Mirror Truth. The times when your reactions to others show you something about yourself. Whether it's what triggers you, what you admire, or what you are resisting, these moments often carry messages about your growing edges.

Prompt 33: When Connection Deepens. These are the precious times when relationships shift to new levels of authenticity. When something allows you to be more accurate with another person, this prompt helps you understand what supports genuine connection.

PERSONAL EVOLUTION

Just as gardens undergo natural transformations through seasons, our inner worlds constantly evolve and reshape themselves.

Prompt 34: When Old Ways Fall Away: These are the moments when familiar patterns no longer fit. Like outgrowing old clothes, sometimes we notice our usual ways of being feel too small. This prompt helps you navigate times of natural evolution.

Prompt 35: When New Strengths Emerge. These are the times when you surprise yourself with new capabilities, maybe in how you handle a challenge or in what you're able to express. These moments show you your growing edges in beautiful ways.

Prompt 36: When Identity Shifts. Those profound times when you sense yourself becoming someone new. Not through force or effort but through natural evolution. This prompt helps you honor these times of transformation.

TIMES OF CHALLENGE AND RESILIENCE

Life sometimes presents moments that test our strength, like storms revealing how deep our roots are. These prompts help us understand what supports us during difficult times.

Prompt 37: When Courage Surprises You. Those unexpected moments when strength emerges naturally. Times when you handle something you thought might break you and discover new capacities within yourself.

Prompt 38: When Resilience Shows Up. The times when you bounce back from setbacks in ways that surprise you. These moments often reveal inner resources you didn't know you had.

Prompt 39: When Fear Transforms. Those times when facing something scary leads to unexpected growth. When what initially feels threatening becomes a doorway to new understanding.

CYCLES OF RELEASE AND RENEWAL

Like a garden moving through seasons, our lives have natural cycles of letting go and beginning again.

Prompt 40: When It's Time to Let Go. Those moments when you recognize something has served its purpose. Maybe it's a belief, a habit, or a way of being that once protected you but now limits growth.

Prompt 41: When New Beginnings Call. The times when you feel ready to start fresh. When something in you knows it's time to turn a new page, even if the whole story isn't clear yet.

Prompt 42: When the Old Makes Way for New. Those transition times when you're between what was and what will be. Like a garden in early spring, when old growth makes room for new possibilities.

JOY AND SIMPLE PLEASURES

Sometimes, our deepest wisdom comes through moments of natural delight, like sunlight breaking through clouds.

Prompt 43: When Joy Catches You. Those unexpected moments of pure happiness, the times when delight finds you without trying, showing you what naturally lights you up.

Prompt 44: When Simple Things Delight. The times when ordinary moments suddenly feel sacred. When making tea, watching leaves dance, or sharing a laugh reveals the beauty in everyday life.

Prompt 45: When Play Feels Right. Those moments when your playful spirit emerges naturally. When you remember how to enjoy life without making it complicated.

CHOICE AND DECISION POINTS

Life often presents crossroads that ask us to listen deeply to our own knowing.

Prompt 46: When Small Choices Speak Loudly. Those seemingly minor decisions that carry a deeper meaning. The daily choices that reveal what truly matters to you.

Prompt 47: When Your Path Diverges. The times when you sense it's moment to take a different direction. When something in you knows it's time to follow your own star.

Prompt 48: When Clarity Emerges. Those moments when the right path suddenly becomes clear. Not through force or analysis but through quiet knowing.

LEARNING THROUGH EXPERIENCE

Life offers constant invitations to grow, like a garden teaching us through each season's unique challenges and gifts.

Prompt 49: When Mistakes Bring Wisdom. These are the moments when things don't go as planned but leave you richer in understanding. What feels like a failure at the moment opens doors to deeper knowledge.

Prompt 50: When Understanding Deepens. The times when you suddenly see something familiar in a completely new way. Like looking at your garden in a different light and noticing details you'd never seen before.

Prompt 51: When Life Teaches Gently. Those quiet moments of realization that come not through struggle but through simple awareness. When wisdom arrives like morning dew, without effort.

GIVING AND RECEIVING

Our relationships with giving and receiving often reveal deep truths about how we value ourselves and others.

Prompt 52: When Receiving Feels New. Those moments when accepting help or kindness bring up unexpected feelings. When someone's generosity invites you to examine your own worth.

Prompt 53: When Giving Flows Naturally. The times when sharing your gifts feels effortless and right. When generosity springs from genuine abundance rather than obligation.

Prompt 54: When Balance Shifts. Those moments when you recognize the need to adjust the flow between giving and receiving. When life invites you to restore harmony by exchanging energy with others,

SELF-DISCOVERY IN QUIET MOMENTS

Sometimes, our deepest insights come when we're not looking for them, like finding unexpected treasures while simply tending our garden.

Prompt 55: When Silence Speaks. Those times when quiet moments reveal unexpected clarity. When simply being still allows wisdom to surface naturally.

Prompt 56: When Nature Mirrors Truth. The moments when something in the natural world reflects your inner experience. When a sunset, a flower, or a bird's flight carries a message just for you.

Prompt 57: When Time Feels Different. Those experiences when you lose track of clock time because something has captured your complete attention. These moments often show you what truly engages your spirit.

CONNECTION AND BELONGING

Our need for authentic connection reveals itself in both subtle and profound ways.

Prompt 58: When Understanding Bridges Gaps. Those precious moments when real understanding flows between people. When differences fade in the light of shared humanity.

Prompt 59: When Community Holds You. The times when you feel genuinely supported by others. When belonging feels natural and authentic rather than something you have to earn.

Prompt 60: When Walls Come Down. Those vulnerable moments when you allow others to see your authentic self. When trust overcomes fear, the actual connection becomes possible.

FINDING YOUR RHYTHM

Life invites us to find our own natural pace and way of being, like each plant in a garden, which has its unique timing for growth and bloom.

Prompt 61: When Flow Finds You. Those moments when everything feels naturally aligned. When your actions, thoughts, and feelings all move in harmony without effort.

Prompt 62: When Your Pace Feels Right. The times when you honor your natural rhythm instead of forcing someone else's timing. When you trust your own way of moving through life.

Prompt 63: When Rest and Action Balance. These are the moments when you find the sweet spot between doing and being when effort and ease dance together perfectly.

EMBRACING THE JOURNEY

Prompt 64: When the Path Surprises. Those times when life takes an unexpected turn that later reveals its wisdom. When what looks like a detour turns out to be the way forward.

Prompt 65: When Now Feels Complete. The moments when you feel fully present and at peace with where you are. When your journey feels perfect exactly as it is, even in its incompleteness.

Each of these prompts offers a unique window into understanding yourself more deeply. Like having different tools in a garden, they help you tend to various aspects of your inner landscape with care and wisdom. Use them when particular moments call for their specific kind of insight, trusting that the right prompt will be there when you need it.

WALKING WITH THESE PROMPTS

You know how certain friends seem to know just what to say in different situations. The ones who can help you see things more clearly just by asking the right questions at the right time? Think of these prompts as those kinds of friends, ready to help you understand whatever life presents more deeply.

Sarah discovered how these prompts could transform challenging moments: "What surprised me most was how having these prompts changed my relationship with difficult situations. Instead of getting caught in old reactions, I found myself getting curious. When praise made me uncomfortable or when saying 'No' felt harder than it should, these prompts helped me understand what was really happening. It's like having a wise friend in your pocket, ready to help you look beneath the surface of any moment."

James found the prompts particularly helpful during times of change: "These prompts became like trusted companions during uncertain times. When old patterns surfaced or when growth felt scary, having these questions helped me stay with the experience long enough to learn from it. I started seeing how every situation, even the uncomfortable ones, carried gifts of understanding if I knew how to unwrap them."

Think about how a garden reveals different aspects of itself in various conditions. Some plants show strength in storms, others show beauty in morning light, and others show resilience through changing seasons. Our inner landscape is similar. Different moments reveal different aspects of who we are and who we're becoming.

These prompts help us recognize and understand these revealing moments. Whether it's a time when joy catches you by surprise, when your body tries to tell you something important, when an old pattern suddenly becomes clear, or when growth asks you to leave familiar territory, there's a prompt here to help you explore that experience more deeply.

Remember, you don't need to use every prompt or understand everything all at once. Like having different tools in your garden shed, these prompts are here when specific situations call for their particular kind of insight. Trust your intuition about which prompt feels right for different moments.

Sarah reflects on how her relationship with the prompts evolved: "At first, I tried to memorize them all, worried I wouldn't have the right one when I needed it. However, I learned that the needed prompts tend to find me naturally. Sometimes, it's through a feeling in my body; other times, through a pattern I notice repeating. The key was learning to trust that the right prompt will be there when I need a certain understanding."

James shares how these prompts changed his way of meeting life's moments: "These prompts taught me that every experience carries wisdom if we know how to listen. Even the challenging times, especially those times, offer opportunities to understand ourselves more deeply. It's not about getting it perfect. It's about staying curious about whatever shows up."

As you move forward with these prompts as your companions, remember that self-discovery isn't about reaching a destination. It's about developing a richer, more nuanced relationship with your own experience. Let these prompts help you explore the countless meaningful moments that make up your journey.

Think of them as friends waiting to help you understand whatever arises, whether it's a moment of challenge or celebration, growth or reflection, connection or solitude. Trust that the right prompt will be there when you need it, helping you unwrap the wisdom each moment brings.

Your journey continues and these prompts go with you, ready to help you discover the deeper meaning in life's many meaningful moments. Keep them close, like trusted friends who know just what to ask when understanding feels most precious.

SEVEN

FINDING YOUR WAY FORWARD

YOUR JOURNEY CONTINUES

Do you know how sometimes the most meaningful conversations leave you satisfied and curious for more? That's often how self-discovery works. Each insight opens new doors, each understanding leads to fresh questions, and each revelation invites deeper exploration.

Looking back over these prompts, you might notice how they build upon each other naturally. The daily prompts help you notice life's quiet whispers. Weekly reflection reveals patterns in those whispers, showing the themes running through your days. Monthly deep dives illuminate the larger seasons of your growth. And those situational prompts? They're there for those special moments when life asks something particular of you.

THE GIFTS OF REGULAR PRACTICE

Think about how a garden changes when you tend it regularly. Each small act of care contributes to its overall flourishing.

Your journal practice works the same way. Every entry, whether a few lines or several pages, adds to your understanding of yourself.

Daily moments of reflection become like morning light, gently illuminating what needs attention. Weekly pauses allow you to notice patterns, like watching how different plants grow together. Monthly deep dives give you that broader view, helping you understand the seasons of your life. Those situational prompts stand ready, like trusted friends, when specific moments call for their particular wisdom.

CREATING YOUR OWN WAY

Remember those historical figures we met at the beginning? Each one found a unique way to use journaling to gain a deeper understanding. Marcus Aurelius wrote to strengthen his principles, Virginia Woolf explored her creativity, and Anne Frank found light in the darkness. Their journals were as different as their lives, yet each served a vital purpose.

Your practice will also be uniquely yours. You might discover that early mornings work best for reflection, or perhaps evening reviews feel more natural. You might find yourself drawn to certain prompts more than others or notice that different types of reflection serve you in different seasons.

Trust this natural evolution. Your relationship with these prompts will grow and change as you do. Some days might bring profound insights, others quiet observations. Both serve your growth.

NURTURING CONTINUOUS DISCOVERY

As you continue this journey, consider how you might weave reflection naturally into your life:

- **Quiet Moments**: Let daily pauses become like taking deep breaths, natural spaces to check in with yourself.
- **Weekly Windows**: Create gentle rhythms for looking back over your days, noticing what patterns want your attention.
- **Monthly Meaning**: Allow these deeper reflections to help you understand the larger stories unfolding in your life.
- **Special Situations**: Keep those situational prompts close, like wise friends ready to help you understand life's meaningful moments.

THE PATH AHEAD

Your journal becomes more valuable over time, like a garden that grows richer with each season of care. It holds your stories, witnesses your growth, and offers space for continuous discovery.

As your practice deepens, you might find yourself noticing subtle shifts in how you meet life's moments, recognizing patterns more quickly and clearly, understanding your needs and values more deeply and trusting your inner wisdom more naturally.

Remember that this journey isn't about reaching a destination or finding perfect answers. It's about developing an ever-deepening relationship with yourself through honest reflection. Each entry adds to your understanding, each question opens new possibilities, and each moment of clarity lights the way forward.

A CONTINUING CONVERSATION

Think of your journal as an ongoing conversation with yourself, one that grows richer and deeper over time. Like those historical journal keepers we met initially, you're creating something unique and valuable. Your journal is not just a record of your days but a map of your inner landscape, a companion for your journey, and a witness to your growth.

Trust that you have everything you need for this exploration. Your curiosity, willingness to examine your experience honestly, and desire to understand yourself more deeply are the only requirements for meaningful self-discovery.

Keep writing, keep wondering, and keep showing up for this conversation with yourself. Each blank page offers a fresh invitation to understand yourself more deeply, grow more fully into who you are, and discover what wisdom awaits in your own experience.

Your journey continues one reflection at a time. And like any good conversation with a trusted friend, there's always more to explore, understand, and discover.

APPENDIX I: RESOURCES FOR DEEPER EXPLORATION

You know how one meaningful conversation often leads to another. As your journaling practice grows, you might find yourself curious about different approaches or wanting to explore specific aspects more deeply. Here are some carefully chosen resources to support your ongoing journey of self-discovery.

BOOKS THAT OPEN NEW DOORS

Think of these books as wise companions for different aspects of your journey. Each offers unique insights into self-discovery through writing.

Understanding the Power of Writing

"Opening Up by Writing It Down" by James Pennebaker and Joshua Smyth is like conversing with researchers who've spent years understanding how writing helps us heal and grow. They share fascinating insights about why putting our thoughts on paper can be so transformative.

"Writing Down the Bones" by Natalie Goldberg. Imagine sitting with a wise writing teacher who understands that honest writing and self-discovery go hand in hand. Goldberg's approach helps you write more freely and authentically.

Deepening Your Practice

"The Artist's Way" by Julia Cameron is more than just a book. It is like having a creative mentor who understands how self-discovery and creative expression naturally support each other. Her morning pages practice has helped countless people develop deeper self-awareness.

"At a Journal Workshop" by Ira Progoff. Think of this as an advanced guide for when you're ready to explore the deeper waters of journal writing. Progoff's intensive journal method offers structured ways to understand your life's patterns and meanings.

"Write Your Way" by Richard French. A comprehensive guide that bridges personal growth and self-expression through journaling. This book helps you master specialized journaling methods, transform personal entries into deeper insights, and develop emotional intelligence through focused practice.

Additional Books in the Journaling Mastery Series

"The Art of Journaling: A Comprehensive Guide to Writing a Journal". Perfect for building strong foundations in your practice. This guide helps you select the right tools, break through common barriers, and blend journaling with mindfulness practices.

"The Year End Reflection Guide: A Write Your Way Bonus." Transform your yearly review with the Five Phase Reflection Framework, helping you gather experiences, identify patterns, and create robust action plans for the future.

"Advanced Pattern Recognition: An Art of Journaling Bonus Guide". Take your practice deeper with the innovative Meta Pattern Framework, helping you map connections in your life and create templates for positive change.

DIGITAL TOOLS FOR MODERN PRACTICE

While pen and paper have a special quality, digital tools can offer unique ways to support your practice.

Journal Apps

- Day One: Perfect for those who want to include photos and location details in their reflections
- Penzu: Focuses on privacy and security for those who value confidentiality
- Journey: Combines beautiful design with practical features for regular reflection

Mindfulness Apps That Complement Journaling

- Insight Timer: Offers guided meditations that can help you center before writing
- Calm: Provides peaceful sounds and mindfulness exercises that enhance reflection

FINDING COMMUNITY

Sometimes, sharing the journey with others can deepen your practice while maintaining your personal reflections' privacy.

Online Spaces

- Reddit's r/journaling: A welcoming community sharing techniques and inspiration
- Journaling.com Forums: Connect with others exploring self-discovery through writing
- Goodreads Journaling Groups: Discuss books about journaling and share experiences

Local Connections

Consider looking for:

- Writing circles at local libraries
- Mindfulness groups that incorporate journaling
- Creative writing workshops that welcome personal reflection

COMPLEMENTARY PRACTICES

Like different plants supporting each other in a garden, these practices can enhance your journaling journey.

Movement and Awareness

- Walking meditation: Combining gentle movement with reflection
- Nature journaling: Using the natural world to inspire deeper awareness
- Body scan practices: Understanding the wisdom of physical sensations

Creative Expression

- Art journaling: Adding visual elements to your written reflection

- Poetry for personal discovery: Using metaphor and imagery to explore inner experiences
- Collage journaling: Combining images and words for deeper insight

WHEN YOU NEED SUPPORT

Remember that deep self-discovery sometimes stirs up challenging emotions. It's wise to know where to find professional support if needed:

- Local counseling services
- Art therapists who work with journaling
- Mindfulness teachers who understand personal growth work
- Writing therapists who specialize in therapeutic writing

CREATING YOUR RESOURCE GARDEN

Think of these resources as different plants in your garden of self-discovery. Some might call for your attention right away, while others might be perfect for future seasons of growth. Trust your intuition about what supports you best right now.

Remember that, like any good conversation, your relationship with these resources will evolve naturally. Let them inspire and support you without feeling pressure to use them all. Your journey is unique, and you'll know which tools and practices feel right for different moments along the way.

APPENDIX II: UNDERSTANDING THE SCIENCE OF SELF-DISCOVERY

Isn't it fascinating how something as simple as writing down our thoughts can create meaningful change in our lives? While people have known this intuitively for centuries - just think about Marcus Aurelius writing his meditations by candlelight - modern research has helped us understand why this practice can be so transformative.

HOW WRITING CHANGES US

When researchers like James Pennebaker began studying the effects of expressive writing, they discovered something remarkable. People who wrote about their experiences didn't just feel better - their physical health improved, their stress levels dropped, and they gained clearer insight into their lives.

Think about what happens when you write about something that matters to you. Your mind naturally organizes the experience. You start noticing patterns you might have missed. Sometimes, you even find meaning in situations that previously felt confusing or overwhelming. This isn't just your imagination - it's your brain doing what it does best: making sense of your experience.

THE SCIENCE BEHIND THE MAGIC

Research shows that regular journaling can:

- Help us process emotional experiences more effectively
- Reduce stress by giving us a healthy way to explore our feelings
- Improve our decision making by helping us see situations more clearly
- Strengthen our self-awareness by revealing patterns in our thoughts and behaviors
- Enhance our creativity by giving our ideas space to develop

However, the most interesting finding may be how journaling helps bridge the gap between our emotional and rational minds. When we write, we engage both the feeling and thinking parts of ourselves. This integration helps us understand our experiences more fully and respond to life's challenges with greater wisdom.

DIFFERENT WAYS OF KNOWING

Think about how different people in history have used journaling. Virginia Woolf explored her creativity through stream-of-consciousness writing. Benjamin Franklin tracked his progress on specific virtues he wanted to develop. Frida Kahlo combined words and images to understand her experience.

Modern research suggests there's no "right" way to journal. What matters is finding approaches that help you:

- Express yourself honestly
- Reflect on your experiences
- Notice patterns in your life
- Explore possibilities for growth

Studies show that even brief periods of reflective writing can lead to meaningful insights. Sometimes, just a few minutes of honest reflection can help us see things in new ways.

WHEN WRITING HEALS

Some of the most fascinating research examines how journaling can help us navigate challenging times. Studies have found that writing about difficult experiences can:

- Reduce symptoms of anxiety and depression
- Help us process grief and loss
- Support us through major life transitions
- Assist in healing from past trauma

But here's something important to remember: while journaling can be incredibly helpful, it works best as part of a balanced approach to well-being. Sometimes, we might need additional support, especially when exploring challenging emotions or experiences.

THE BODY-MIND CONNECTION

Recent research has revealed interesting connections between writing and physical well-being. Regular journaling has been associated with:

- Improved immune system functioning
- Better sleep quality
- Reduced symptoms of stress
- Enhanced overall well-being

This mind-body connection isn't surprising when you think about it. Our thoughts, feelings, and physical experiences are all interconnected. Writing gives us a way to work with this connection consciously and constructively.

MAKING IT WORK FOR YOU

While research provides valuable insights into journaling's benefits, remember that your experience is unique. What matters most is finding ways of reflecting that feel genuine and helpful to you.

Some people discover that:

- Morning writing helps them start the day with clarity
- Evening reflection helps them process and integrate their experiences
- Weekly reviews help them notice patterns and make adjustments
- Combining writing with other practices like meditation enhances both

The key is to remain curious about what works best for you and to be open to trying new approaches when they seem appropriate.

LOOKING FORWARD

As research continues, we're learning more about how different forms of reflection support personal growth and well-being. But what's most exciting is how this modern understanding confirms what journal-keepers throughout history have known. There's something powerfully transformative about meeting ourselves on the page with honesty and curiosity.

Remember that you're participating in an ancient practice and an evolving understanding of how writing supports human growth and healing. Your journal is more than a place to record your thoughts—it's a space for discovering and creating meaning in your own unique way.

APPENDIX III: COMPLEMENTARY APPROACHES TO SELF-DISCOVERY

You know how certain things naturally go well together, like a warm drink and a good conversation? The same is true with journaling. While writing is powerful on its own, combining it with other practices can deepen your journey of self-discovery in beautiful ways.

MOVEMENT AND REFLECTION

Sometimes, our best insights come when we're in motion. Many journal-keepers have discovered how movement can enhance their practice:

Walking and Writing

Think about Virginia Woolf, who often composed her thoughts during long walks through London. Moving your body can help move your thoughts, too. Try:

- Taking a notebook on your morning walk
- Reflecting on paper after movement

- Using walking meditation to clear your mind before writing

Body Awareness

Our bodies often know things before our minds catch up. Combining physical awareness with writing can reveal deeper insights:

- Notice physical sensations as you write
- Journal about what your body is telling you
- Use movement to unlock stuck thoughts or feelings

Nature Connection

Like many historical journal-keepers, you might find that nature enhances your reflection:

- Write outdoors in different weather
- Use natural objects as prompts for reflection
- Let seasonal changes inspire deeper exploration

CREATIVE EXPRESSION

Writing doesn't just have to be words on a page. Many people find that adding other forms of creativity enriches their practice:

Visual Elements

Think of Frida Kahlo's journals, filled with both words and images. You might try:

- Sketching alongside your writing
- Using colors to express emotions

- Creating collages that complement your words

Poetry and Metaphor

Sometimes, poetic language can express what ordinary words can't:

- Play with imagery and metaphor
- Write simple haiku about your day
- Use poems as prompts for deeper reflection

Musical Connection

Music can help create different moods for reflection:

- Create playlists for different types of writing
- Use music as a prompt for exploration
- Notice how different sounds affect your reflection

MINDFULNESS PRACTICES

Bringing mindful awareness to your journaling can deepen your insights:

Meditation and Writing

A few minutes of quiet meditation before writing can help you:

- Center your thoughts
- Access deeper wisdom
- Notice subtle patterns

Breath Awareness

Your breath can be an anchor for more present reflection:

- Take three deep breaths before writing
- Notice your breathing as you explore difficult topics
- Use breath to pace your reflection

Present Moment Practice

Training yourself to notice the now can enrich your writing:

- Start entries with current sensations
- Describe moments in rich detail
- Practice presence between writing sessions

RITUAL AND RHYTHM

Creating simple rituals around your practice can make it more meaningful.

Sacred Space

Consider how you might make your writing time special:

- Light a candle
- Choose a special place
- Create a small altar with meaningful objects

Time and Timing

Different times of day might serve different kinds of reflection:

- Early morning for fresh insights
- Evening for processing the day
- Afternoon for creative exploration

Seasonal Practice

Let the natural rhythms of the year inform your writing:

- Align reflections with seasons
- Use solstices and equinoxes for a deeper review
- Notice how your practice changes throughout the year

WORKING WITH DREAMS

Dreams can offer rich material for self-discovery:

Dream Journaling

Keeping track of your dreams can reveal interesting patterns:

- Keep a notebook by your bed
- Write dreams before fully waking
- Notice recurring themes

Active Imagination

Try having dialogues with dream images in your journal:

- Write conversations with dream figures
- Explore dream settings through the description
- Let dream images inspire daily reflection

GROUP PRACTICE

While journaling is often solitary, sharing with others can enrich your practice.

Writing Circles

Consider finding or creating a group that supports reflection:

- Share insights (while maintaining privacy)
- Write together in silence

- Explore prompts as a group

Accountability Partners

Having a journaling buddy can help maintain your practice:

- Check-in regularly
- Share what you're learning (not what you're writing)
- Support each other's growth

REMEMBER

These practices are like different spices you might add to enhance a meal. Use what appeals to you, experiment freely, and trust your intuition about what best serves your journey. Some practices might call to you immediately, while others might be perfect for future exploration.

What matters isn't how many practices you combine but how they help you listen more deeply to your own wisdom. Let your curiosity guide you as you discover what enriches your unique way of reflecting and growing.

NOTE FROM THE AUTHOR

Thank you so much for reading. If you enjoyed this book I'd really love it if you could leave a 30 second review on Amazon.

Here is a QR code to the review page.

ABOUT THE AUTHOR

Richard French represents a rare convergence of high-tech leadership, competitive motorsports, and literary achievement. With over 20 years of global C-suite experience, Richard has been recognized as one of the country's foremost authorities on Robotic Process Automation and AI Automation. His executive journey includes senior leadership roles at Oracle and Nokia, CEO positions at multiple successful startups, and the distinction of guiding companies from early-stage ventures to organizations earning over $100 million annually. His expertise spans five continents, where he's built and led teams across diverse markets and cultures.

Beyond the boardroom, Richard channels his passion for precision and performance into GT race car driving, competing across the United States in the Porsche Sprint Challenge Series West. This unique combination of analytical thinking from technology and high-stakes decision-making from racing profoundly influences his approach to writing and leadership philosophy.

Richard's literary portfolio demonstrates remarkable versatility, encompassing his flagship business leadership book *"Daniel as a Blueprint for Navigating Ethical Dilemmas,"* other business ethics guides like *"Proverbs for Profit,"* comprehensive journaling resources including "The Journaling Mastery Series", and *"The Journaling Prompts Series"*, biblical studies such as "*Revelation Explained: Verse by Verse*," and his expansion into speculative fiction with *The Convergence Series*, featuring "*Broken Magic*" and "*Restoration*." His mathematics degree from a top Canadian university and decades of explaining complex technological innovations have honed his ability to make intricate concepts accessible to diverse audiences. Now retired and enjoying the freedom to focus on his passion for writing, Richard lives in the Pacific Northwest with his wife and two Boston Terriers, Reggie and Tilly.

facebook.com/richardfrenchauthor

instagram.com/richardfrenchauthor

tiktok.com/@richardfrenchauthor

youtube.com/@richardfrenchwrites

www.ingramcontent.com/pod-product-compliance
Lightning Source LLC
Chambersburg PA
CBHW071318130626

46556CB00004B/1645